編者的話

　　「學科能力測驗」是「指定科目考試」的前哨站，雖然難度較「指考」低，但是考試內容以及成績，仍然非常具有參考價值，而且「學測」考得好的同學，還可以推甄入學的方式，比別人早一步進入理想的大學，提前放暑假。

　　為了協助考生以最有效率的方式準備大學入學考試，我們特別蒐集了 101 年度「學測」各科試題，包括英文、數學、社會、自然和國文，做成「101 年學科能力測驗各科試題詳解」，書後並附有大考中心所公佈的各科選擇題答案、成績統計表，以及國文、英文兩科非選擇題閱卷評分原則說明。另外，在英文科詳解後面，還附上了英文試題修正意見及英文考科選文出處，讀者可利用空檔時間，上網瀏覽那些網站，增進自己的課外知識，並了解出題方向。

　　這本書的完成，要感謝各科名師全力協助解題：

英文 / 謝靜芳老師・蔡琇瑩老師・褚謙吉老師
　　　林工富老師・蕭雅芳老師・蔡世偉老師
　　　李孟熹老師・李冠勳老師・廖吟倫老師
　　　美籍老師 Laura E. Stewart
　　　　　　　 Christain A. Brieske

數學 / 李卓澔老師

社會 / 李　曄老師・王念平老師・李　易老師

國文 / 李　奐老師

自然 / 張鎮麟老師・王　宇老師・姜孟希老師
　　　殷　琴老師・鄧　翔老師

　　本書編校製作過程嚴謹，但仍恐有缺失之處，尚祈各界先進不吝指正。

劉　毅

CONTENTS

101 年大學入學學科能力測驗試題
英文考科

第壹部分：單選題 (占 72 分)

一、詞彙 (佔 15 分)

說明： 第 1 題至第 15 題，每題有 4 個選項，其中只有一個是正確或最適當的
選項，請畫記在答案卡之「選擇題答案區」。各題答對者，得 1 分；
答錯、未作答或畫記多於一個選項者，該題以零分計算。

1. The ending of the movie did not come as a _____ to John because
   he had already read the novel that the movie was based on.
   (A) vision　　　(B) focus　　　(C) surprise　　　(D) conclusion

2. In order to stay healthy and fit, John exercises _____. He works
   out twice a week in a gym.
   (A) regularly　　(B) directly　　(C) hardly　　　(D) gradually

3. Traveling is a good way for us to _____ different cultures and
   broaden our horizons.
   (A) assume　　　(B) explore　　(C) occupy　　　(D) inspire

4. The story about Hou-I shooting down nine suns is a well-known
   Chinese _____, but it may not be a true historical event.
   (A) figure　　　(B) rumor　　　(C) miracle　　　(D) legend

5. According to recent research, children under the age of 12 are
   generally not _____ enough to recognize risk and deal with
   dangerous situations.
   (A) diligent　　(B) mature　　　(C) familiar　　　(D) sincere

6. Helen let out a sigh of _____ after hearing that her brother was
   not injured in the accident.
   (A) hesitation　　(B) relief　　　(C) sorrow　　　(D) triumph

7. Research suggests that people with outgoing personalities tend to
   be more _____, often expecting that good things will happen.
   (A) efficient　　(B) practical　　(C) changeable　　(D) optimistic

8. No one could beat Paul at running. He has won the running
   championship _____ for three years.
   (A) rapidly　　(B) urgently　　(C) continuously　　(D) temporarily

9. If you fly from Taipei to Tokyo, you'll be taking an international,
   rather than a _____ flight.
   (A) liberal　　(B) domestic　　(C) connected　　(D) universal

10. Jack is very proud of his fancy new motorcycle. He has been _____
    to all his friends about how cool it looks and how fast it runs.
    (A) boasting　　(B) proposing　　(C) gossiping　　(D) confessing

11. The ideas about family have changed _____ in the past twenty
    years. For example, my grandfather was one of ten children in his
    family, but I am the only child.
    (A) mutually　　(B) narrowly　　(C) considerably　　(D) scarcely

12. The chairperson of the meeting asked everyone to speak up instead
    of _____ their opinions among themselves.
    (A) reciting　　(B) giggling　　(C) murmuring　　(D) whistling

13. Although Mr. Chen is rich, he is a very _____ person and is
    never willing to spend any money to help those who are in need.
    (A) absolute　　(B) precise　　(C) economic　　(D) stingy

14. If you want to know what your dreams mean, now there are
    websites you can visit to help you _____ them.
    (A) overcome　　(B) interpret　　(C) transfer　　(D) revise

15. The memory _____ of the new computer has been increased so
    that more information can be stored.
    (A) capacity　　(B) occupation　　(C) attachment　　(D) machinery

二、綜合測驗（占 15 分）

說明： 第 16 題至第 30 題，每題一個空格，請依文意選出最適當的一個選項，
請畫記在答案卡之「選擇題答案區」。各題答對者，得 1 分；答錯、
未作答、或畫記多於一個選項者，該題以零分計算。

Kizhi is an island on Lake Onega in Karelia, Russia, with a beautiful collection of wooden churches and houses. It is one of the most popular tourist __16__ in Russia and a United Nations Educational, Scientific, and Cultural Organization (UNESCO) World Heritage Site.

The island is about 7 km long and 0.5 km wide. It is surrounded by about 5,000 other islands, some of __17__ are just rocks sticking out of the ground.

The entire island of Kizhi is, __18__, an outdoor museum of wooden architecture created in 1966. It contains many historically significant and beautiful wooden structures, __19__ windmills, boathouses, chapels, fish houses, and homes. The jewel of the architecture is the 22-domed Transfiguration Church, built in the early 1700s. It is about 37 m tall, __20__ it one of the tallest log structures in the world. The church was built with pine trees brought from the mainland, which was quite common for the 18th century.

16. (A) affairs   (B) fashions   (C) industries   (D) attractions
17. (A) them   (B) that   (C) those   (D) which
18. (A) in fact   (B) once again   (C) as usual   (D) for instance
19. (A) except   (B) besides   (C) including   (D) regarding
20. (A) make   (B) making   (C) made   (D) to make

There was once a time when all human beings were gods. However, they often took their divinity for granted and __21__ abused it. Seeing this, Brahma, the chief god, decided to take their divinity away from them and hide it __22__ it could never be found.

Brahma called a council of the gods to help him decide on a place to hide the divinity. The gods suggested that they hide it ___23___ in the earth or take it to the top of the highest mountain. But Brahma thought ___24___ would do because he believed humans would dig into the earth and climb every mountain, and eventually find it. So, the gods gave up.

Brahma thought for a long time and finally decided to hide their divinity in the center of their own being, for humans would never think to ___25___ it there. Since that time humans have been going up and down the earth, digging, climbing, and exploring—searching for something already within themselves.

21. (A) yet   (B) even   (C) never   (D) rather
22. (A) though   (B) because   (C) where   (D) when
23. (A) close   (B) apart   (C) deep   (D) hard
24. (A) each   (B) more   (C) any   (D) neither
25. (A) look for   (B) get over   (C) do without   (D) bump into

In the fall of 1973, in an effort to bring attention to the conflict between Egypt and Israel, *World Hello Day* was born. The objective is to promote peace all over the world, and to ___26___ barriers between every nationality. Since then, *World Hello Day*—November 21st of every year— ___27___ observed by people in 180 countries.

Taking part couldn't be ___28___. All one has to do is say hello to 10 people on the day. However, in response to the ___29___ of this event, the concepts of fostering peace and harmony do not have to be confined to one day a year. We can ___30___ the spirit going by communicating often and consciously. It is a simple act that anyone can do and it reminds us that communication is more effective than conflict.

26. (A) skip over   (B) come across   (C) look into   (D) break down
27. (A) is   (B) has been   (C) was   (D) had been
28. (A) quicker   (B) sooner   (C) easier   (D) better
29. (A) aim   (B) tone   (C) key   (D) peak
30. (A) push   (B) keep   (C) bring   (D) make

三、文意選填（占 10 分）

說明： 第 31 題至第 40 題，每題一個空格，請依文意在文章後所提供的 (A) 到 (J) 選項中分別選出最適當者，並將其英文字母代號畫記在答案卡之「選擇題答案區」。各題答對者，得 1 分；答錯、未作答或畫記多於一個選項者，該題以零分計算。

Generally there are two ways to name typhoons: the number-based convention and the list-based convention. Following the number-based convention, typhoons are coded with ＿＿31＿＿ types of numbers such as a 4-digit or a 6-digit code. For example, the 14th typhoon in 2003 can be labeled either as Typhoon 0314 or Typhoon 200314. The ＿＿32＿＿ of this convention, however, is that a number is hard to remember. The list-based convention, on the other hand, is based on the list of typhoon names compiled in advance by a committee, and is more widely used.

At the very beginning, only ＿＿33＿＿ names were used because at that time typhoons were named after girlfriends or wives of the experts on the committee. In 1979, however, male names were also included because women protested against the original naming ＿＿34＿＿ for reasons of gender equality.

In Asia, Western names were used until 2000 when the committee decided to use Asian names to ＿＿35＿＿ Asians' awareness of typhoons. The names were chosen from a name pool ＿＿36＿＿ of 140 names, 10 each from the 14 members of the committee. Each country has its unique naming preferences. Korea and Japan ＿＿37＿＿ animal names and China likes names of gods such as Longwang (dragon king) and Fengshen (god of the wind).

After the 140 names are all used in order, they will be ＿＿38＿＿. But the names can be changed. If a member country suffers great damage from a certain typhoon, it can ＿＿39＿＿ that the name of the typhoon be deleted from the list at the annual committee meeting. For example, the names of Nabi by South Korea, and Longwang by China were ＿＿40＿＿

with other names in 2007. The deletion of both names was due to the severe damage caused by the typhoons bearing the names.

(A) request   (B) favor   (C) disadvantage   (D) composed

(E) recycled   (F) practice   (G) replaced   (H) raise

(I) various   (J) female

四、閱讀測驗（占 32 分）

說明： 第 41 題至第 56 題，每題請分別根據各篇文章之文意選出最適當的一個選項，請畫記在答案卡之「選擇題答案區」。各題答對者，得 2 分；答錯、未作答或畫記多於一個選項者，該題以零分計算。

41-44 為題組

The kilt is a skirt traditionally worn by Scottish men. It is a tailored garment that is wrapped around the wearer's body at the waist starting from one side, around the front and back and across the front again to the opposite side. The overlapping layers in front are called "aprons." Usually, the kilt covers the body from the waist down to just above the knees. A properly made kilt should not be so loose that the wearer can easily twist the kilt around the body, nor should it be so tight that it causes bulging of the fabric where it is buckled. Underwear may be worn as one prefers.

One of the most distinctive features of the kilt is the pattern of squares, or sett, it exhibits. The association of particular patterns with individual families can be traced back hundreds of years. Then in the Victorian era (19th century), weaving companies began to systematically record and formalize the system of setts for commercial purposes. Today there are also setts for States and Provinces, schools and universities, and general patterns that anybody can wear.

The kilt can be worn with accessories. On the front apron, there is often a kilt pin, topped with a small decorative family symbol. A small knife can be worn with the kilt too. It typically comes in a very wide variety, from fairly plain to quite elaborate silver- and jewel-ornamented designs. The kilt can also be worn with a sporran, which is the Gaelic word for pouch or purse.

41. What's the proper way of wearing the kilt?
    (A) It should be worn with underwear underneath it.
    (B) It should loosely fit on the body to be turned around.
    (C) It should be long enough to cover the wearer's knees.
    (D) It should be wrapped across the front of the body two times.

42. Which of the following is a correct description about setts?
    (A) They were once symbols for different Scottish families.
    (B) They were established by the government for business purposes.
    (C) They represented different States and Provinces in the 19th century.
    (D) They used to come in one general pattern for all individuals and institutions.

43. Which of the following items is NOT typically worn with the kilt for decoration?
    (A) A pin.   (B) A purse.
    (C) A ruby apron.   (D) A silver knife.

44. What is the purpose of this passage?
    (A) To introduce a Scottish garment.
    (B) To advertise a weaving pattern.
    (C) To persuade men to wear kilts.
    (D) To compare a skirt with a kilt.

45-48 為題組

Wesla Whitfield, a famous jazz singer, has a unique style and life story, so I decided to see one of her performances and interview her for my column.

I went to a nightclub in New York and watched the stage lights go up. After the band played an introduction, Wesla Whitfield wheeled herself onstage in a wheelchair. As she sang, Whitfield's voice was so powerful and soulful that everyone in the room forgot the wheelchair was even there.

At 57, Whitfield is small and pretty, witty and humble, persistent and philosophical. Raised in California, Whitfield began performing in public at age 18, when she took a job as a singing waitress at a pizza parlor. After studying classical music in college, she moved to San Francisco and went on to sing with the San Francisco Opera Chorus.

Walking home from rehearsal at age 29, she was caught in the midst of a random shooting that left her paralyzed from the waist down. I asked how she dealt with the realization that she'd never walk again, and she confessed that initially she didn't want to face it. After a year of depression she tried to kill herself. She was then admitted to a hospital for treatment, where she was able to recover.

Whitfield said she came to understand that the only thing she had lost in this misfortunate event was the ability to walk. She still possessed her most valuable asset—her mind. Pointing to her head, she said, "Everything important is in here. The only real disability in life is losing your mind." When I asked if she was angry about what she had lost, she admitted to being frustrated occasionally, "especially when everybody's dancing, because I love to dance. But **when that happens** I just remove myself so I can focus instead on what I can do."

45. In which of the following places has Wesla Whitfield worked?
    (A) A college.   (B) A hospital.
    (C) A pizza parlor.   (D) A news agency.

46. What does "**when that happens**" mean in the last paragraph?
    (A) When Wesla is losing her mind.
    (B) When Wesla is singing on the stage.
    (C) When Wesla is going out in her wheelchair.
    (D) When Wesla is watching other people dancing.

47. Which of the following statements is true about Wesla Whitfield's
    physical disability?
    (A) It was caused by a traffic accident.
    (B) It made her sad and depressed at first.
    (C) It seriously affected her singing career.
    (D) It happened when she was a college student.

48. What advice would Wesla most likely give other disabled people?
    (A) Ignore what you have lost and make the best use of what you
        have.
    (B) Be modest and hard-working to earn respect from other people.
    (C) Acquire a skill so that you can still be successful and famous.
    (D) Try to sing whenever you feel upset and depressed.

49-52 為題組

　　Forks trace their origins back to the ancient Greeks. Forks at that
time were fairly large with two tines that aided in the carving of meat in
the kitchen. The tines prevented meat from twisting or moving during
carving and allowed food to slide off more easily than it would with a
knife.

　　By the 7th century A.D., royal courts of the Middle East began to
use forks at the table for dining. From the 10th through the 13th centuries,
forks were fairly common among the wealthy in Byzantium. In the 11th
century, a Byzantine wife brought forks to Italy; however, they were not

widely adopted there until the 16th century. Then in 1533, forks were brought from Italy to France. The French were also slow to accept forks, for using them was thought to be awkward.

In 1608, forks were brought to England by Thomas Coryate, who saw them during his travels in Italy. The English first ridiculed forks as being unnecessary. "Why should a person need a fork when God had given him hands?" they asked. Slowly, however, forks came to be adopted by the wealthy as a symbol of their social status. They were prized possessions made of expensive materials intended to impress guests. By the mid 1600s, eating with forks was considered fashionable among the wealthy British.

Early table forks were modeled after kitchen forks, but small pieces of food often fell through the two tines or slipped off easily. In late 17th century France, larger forks with four curved tines were developed. The additional tines made diners less likely to drop food, and the curved tines served as a scoop so people did not have to constantly switch to a spoon while eating. By the early 19th century, four-tined forks had also been developed in Germany and England and slowly began to spread to America.

49. What is the passage mainly about?
    (A) The different designs of forks.
    (B) The spread of fork-aided cooking.
    (C) The history of using forks for dining.
    (D) The development of fork-related table manners.

50. By which route did the use of forks spread?
    (A) Middle East→Greece→England→Italy→France
    (B) Greece→Middle East→Italy→France→England

(C) Greece→Middle East→France→Italy→Germany

(D) Middle East→France→England→Italy→Germany

51. How did forks become popular in England?

(A) Wealthy British were impressed by the design of forks.

(B) Wealthy British thought it awkward to use their hands to eat.

(C) Wealthy British gave special forks to the nobles as luxurious gifts.

(D) Wealthy British considered dining with forks a sign of social status.

52. Why were forks made into a curved shape?

(A) They could be used to scoop food as well.

(B) They looked more fashionable in this way.

(C) They were designed in this way for export to the US.

(D) They ensured the meat would not twist while being cut.

53-56 為題組

Animals are a favorite subject of many photographers. Cats, dogs, and other pets top the list, followed by zoo animals. However, because it's hard to get them to sit still and "perform on command," some professional photographers refuse to photograph pets.

One way to get an appealing portrait of a cat or dog is to hold a biscuit or treat above the camera. The animal's longing look toward the food will be captured by the camera, but the treat won't appear in the picture because it's out of the camera's range. When you show the picture to your friends afterwards, they'll be impressed by your pet's loving expression.

If you are using fast film, you can take some good, quick shots of a pet by simply snapping a picture right after calling its name. You'll get a different expression from your pet using this technique. Depending on your pet's mood, the picture will capture an interested, curious expression or possibly a look of annoyance, especially if you've awakened it from a nap. Taking pictures of zoo animals requires a little more patience. After all, you can't wake up a lion! You may have to wait for a while until the animal does something interesting or moves into a position for you to get a good shot. When photographing zoo animals, don't get too close to the cages, and never tap on the glass or throw things between the bars of a cage. Concentrate on shooting some good pictures, and always respect the animals you are photographing.

53. Why do some professional photographers NOT like to take pictures of pets?
    (A) Pets may not follow orders.
    (B) Pets don't want to be bothered.
    (C) Pets may not like photographers.
    (D) Pets seldom change their expressions.

54. What is the use of a biscuit in taking pictures of a pet?
    (A) To capture a cute look.
    (B) To create a special atmosphere.
    (C) To arouse the appetite of the pet.
    (D) To keep the pet from looking at the camera.

55. What is the advantage of calling your pet's name when taking a shot of it?
    (A) To help your pet look its best.
    (B) To make sure that your pet sits still.
    (C) To keep your pet awake for a while.
    (D) To catch a different expression of your pet.

56. In what way is photographing zoo animals different from photographing pets?
   (A) You need to have fast film.
   (B) You need special equipment.
   (C) You need to stay close to the animals.
   (D) You need more time to watch and wait.

第貳部份：非選擇題（占 28 分）

一、中譯英（占 8 分）

說明： 1. 請將以下中文句子譯成正確、通順、達意的英文，並將答案寫在「答案卷」上。
   2. 請依序作答，並標明題號。每題 4 分，共 8 分。

1. 近年來，許多臺灣製作的影片已經受到國際的重視。
2. 拍攝這些電影的地點也成為熱門的觀光景點。

二、英文作文（占 20 分）

說明： 1. 依提示在「答案卷」上寫一篇英文作文。
   2. 文長至少 120 個單詞（words）。

提示：你最好的朋友最近迷上電玩，因此常常熬夜，疏忽課業，並受到父母的責罵。你（英文名字必須假設為 Jack 或 Jill）打算寫一封信給他/她（英文名字必須假設為 Ken 或 Barbie），適當地給予勸告。

請注意：必須使用上述的 Jack 或 Jill 在信末署名，**不得使用自己的真實中文或英文名字**。

101年度學科能力測驗英文科試題詳解

第壹部分：單選題

一、詞彙：

1. (**C**) The ending of the movie did not come as a <u>surprise</u> to John because he had already read the novel that the movie was based on.
這部電影的結局約翰並不<u>驚訝</u>，因爲他已經看過這部電影的原著小說。
(A) vision (ˈvɪʒən) *n.* 視力
(B) focus (ˈfokəs) *n.* 焦點
(C) ***surprise*** (səˈpraɪz) *n.* 驚訝
(D) conclusion (kənˈkluʒən) *n.* 結論
be based on 以～爲基礎

2. (**A**) In order to stay healthy and fit, John exercises <u>regularly</u>. He works out twice a week in a gym.
爲了保持健康，約翰<u>規律</u>運動。他一個禮拜去健身房運動兩次。
(A) ***regularly*** (ˈrɛgjələ‧lɪ) *adv.* 規律地
(B) directly (dəˈrɛktlɪ) *adv.* 直接地
(C) hardly (ˈhɑrdlɪ) *adv.* 幾乎不
(D) gradually (ˈgrædʒʊəlɪ) *adv.* 逐漸地
fit (fɪt) *adj.* 健康的　　***work out*** 運動　　gym (dʒɪm) *n.* 健身房

3. (**B**) Traveling is a good way for us to <u>explore</u> different cultures and broaden our horizons.
旅行是個使我們<u>探索</u>不同文化和拓展視野的好方法。
(A) assume (əˈsjum) *v.* 假設
(B) ***explore*** (ɪkˈsplor) *v.* 探索
(C) occupy (ˈɑkjə‧paɪ) *v.* 佔據
(D) inspire (ɪnˈspaɪr) *v.* 激勵
culture (ˈkʌltʃə‧) *n.* 文化　　broaden (ˈbrɔdn̩) *v.* 拓展
horizons (həˈraɪzn̩z) *n. pl.* 知識範圍

4. (**D**) The story about Hou-I shooting down nine suns is a well-known Chinese underline{legend}, but it may not be a true historical event.
關於后羿射下九個太陽的故事，是中國著名的底線{傳說}，但是它可能不是眞正的歷史事件。

(A) figure〔'fɪgjɚ〕*n.* 人物
(B) rumor〔'rumɚ〕*n.* 謠言
(C) miracle〔'mɪrəkl̩〕*n.* 奇蹟
(D) **legend**〔'lɛdʒənd〕*n.* 傳說

shoot down 射下　　well-known〔'wɛl'nɔn〕*adj.* 著名的
historical〔hɪs'tɔrɪkl̩〕*adj.* 歷史的　　event〔ɪ'vɛnt〕*n.* 事件

5. (**B**) According to recent research, children under the age of 12 are generally not underline{mature} enough to recognize risk and deal with dangerous situations. 根據最近的研究，十二歲以下的孩童通常還沒底線{成熟}到可以認清危險，以及處理危險的情況。

(A) diligent〔'dɪlədʒənt〕*adj.* 勤勉的
(B) **mature**〔mə'tʃʊr〕*adj.* 成熟的　　(C) familiar〔fə'mɪljɚ〕*adj.* 熟悉的
(D) sincere〔sɪn'sɪr〕*adj.* 眞誠的

recent〔'risn̩t〕*adj.* 最近的　　research〔rɪ's³tʃ〕*n.* 研究
recognize〔'rɛkəg͵naɪz〕*v.* 認出　　risk〔rɪsk〕*n.* 危險
deal with 處理　　situation〔͵sɪtʃʊ'eʃən〕*n.* 情況

6. (**B**) Helen let out a sigh of underline{relief} after hearing that her brother was not injured in the accident.
海倫聽到她的哥哥在這場意外中沒有受傷之後，鬆了一口氣。

(A) hesitation〔͵hɛzə'teʃən〕*n.* 猶豫
(B) **relief**〔rɪ'lif〕*n.* 放心；鬆了一口氣
(C) sorrow〔'saro〕*n.* 傷心　　(D) triumph〔'traɪəmf〕*n.* 勝利

let out 發出　　sigh〔saɪ〕*n.* 嘆氣
injure〔'ɪndʒɚ〕*v.* 傷害；使受傷　　accident〔'æksədənt〕*n.* 意外

7. (**D**) Research suggests that people with outgoing personalities tend to be more underline{optimistic}, often expecting that good things will happen.
研究指出，個性外向的人通常比較底線{樂觀}，常認爲會有好事發生。

(A) efficient〔ɪ'fɪʃənt〕*adj.* 有效率的
(B) practical〔'præktɪkl̩〕*adj.* 實際的
(C) changeable〔'tʃendʒəbl̩〕*adj.* 多變的
(D) **optimistic**〔͵ɑptə'mɪstɪk〕*adj.* 樂觀的

suggest〔sə'dʒɛst〕v. 顯示　　outgoing〔'aʊt,goɪŋ〕adj. 外向的
personality〔,pɜsn̩'æləti〕n. 個性　　***tend to V.*** 傾向於～
expect〔ɪk'spɛkt〕v. 期待；預計會有

8.(**C**) No one could beat Paul at running. He has won the running
championship <u>continuously</u> for three years.
在跑步方面，無人能擊敗保羅。他已經<u>連續</u>三年贏得跑步冠軍了。
(A) rapidly〔'ræpɪdlɪ〕adv. 快速地
(B) urgently〔'ɜdʒəntlɪ〕adv. 迫切地
(C) ***continuously***〔kən'tɪnjʊəslɪ〕adv. 連續地
(D) temporarily〔'tɛmpə,rɛrəlɪ〕adv. 暫時地
beat〔bit〕v. 打敗　　championship〔'tʃæmpɪən,ʃɪp〕n. 冠軍（資格）

9.(**B**) If you fly from Taipei to Tokyo, you'll be taking an international,
rather than a <u>domestic</u> flight.
如果你搭飛機從台北飛到東京，你將會搭乘國際航班，而非<u>國內</u>航班。
(A) liberal〔'lɪbərəl〕adj. 自由的
(B) ***domestic***〔də'mɛstɪk〕adj. 國內的
(C) connected〔kə'nɛktɪd〕adj. 連結的
(D) universal〔,junə'vɜsl̩〕adj. 全球的
fly〔flaɪ〕v. 搭飛機　　international〔,ɪntə'næʃənl̩〕adj. 國際的
rather than 而非　　flight〔flaɪt〕n. 班機

10.(**A**) Jack is very proud of his fancy new motorcycle. He has been
<u>boasting</u> to all his friends about how cool it looks and how fast it
runs. 傑克對於他的酷炫新摩托車感到非常驕傲。他一直向他所有
的朋友<u>誇耀</u>它有多酷，它能跑多快。
(A) ***boast***〔bost〕v. 誇耀　　(B) propose〔prə'poz〕v. 提議
(C) gossip〔'gɑsəp〕v. 說閒話　n. 八卦
(D) confess〔kən'fɛs〕v. 招認
be proud of 以～為榮
fancy〔'fænsɪ〕adj. 昂貴的；花俏的；酷炫的

11.(**C**) The ideas about family have changed <u>considerably</u> in the past
twenty years. For example, my grandfather was one of ten
children in his family, but I am the only child.
家庭的觀念在過去二十年來已有<u>相當大</u>的改變。例如，我祖父生長
在一個有十個兄弟姊妹的家庭，但我是家裡的獨生子。

(A) mutually〔'mjutʃuəlɪ〕*adv.* 互相地

(B) narrowly〔'nærolɪ〕*adv.* 狹窄地；勉強地

(C) ***considerably***〔kən'sɪdərəblɪ〕*adv.* 相當大地

(D) scarcely〔'skɛrslɪ〕*adv.* 幾乎不

past〔pæst〕*adj.* 過去的

12. (**C**) The chairperson of the meeting asked everyone to speak up instead of <u>murmuring</u> their opinions among themselves. 會議的主席要求大家大聲說出來，不要彼此之間<u>小聲地說</u>自己的意見。

(A) recite〔rɪ'saɪt〕*v.* 朗誦；背誦　　(B) giggle〔'gɪgl〕*v.* 吃吃地笑

(C) ***murmur***〔'mɝmɚ〕*v.* 喃喃地說：小聲說

(D) whistle〔'hwɪsl〕*v.* 吹口哨

chairperson〔'tʃɛr,pɝsn̩〕*n.* 主席　　***speak up*** 大聲說

opinion〔ə'pɪnjən〕*n.* 意見

13. (**D**) Although Mr. Chen is rich, he is a very <u>stingy</u> person and is never willing to spend any money to help those who are in need.
雖然陳先生很有錢，但他卻是個非常<u>小氣的</u>人，從不願意花任何錢幫助那些貧困的人。

(A) absolute〔'æbsə,lut〕*adj.* 當然的；絕對的

(B) precise〔prɪ'saɪs〕*adj.* 精確的

(C) economic〔,ikə'nɑmɪk〕*adj.* 經濟的

(D) ***stingy***〔'stɪndʒɪ〕*adj.* 小氣的

willing〔'wɪlɪŋ〕*adj.* 願意的　　***in need*** 貧困的

14. (**B**) If you want to know what your dreams mean, now there are websites you can visit to help you <u>interpret</u> them.
如果你想知道你的夢境是什麼意思，現在你可以瀏覽很多網站，幫助你<u>解夢</u>。

(A) overcome〔,ovɚ'kʌm〕*v.* 克服　　(B) ***interpret***〔ɪn'tɝprɪt〕*v.* 解釋

(C) transfer〔træns'fɝ〕*v.* 轉移　　(D) revise〔rɪ'vaɪz〕*v.* 校訂

website〔'wɛb,saɪt〕*n.* 網站

15. (**A**) The memory <u>capacity</u> of the new computer has been increased so that more information can be stored.
新電腦的記憶體容量已經增加，所以可儲存更多的資料。

(A) *capacity*〔kə'pæsətɪ〕*n.* 容量
(B) occupation〔͵ɑkjə'peʃən〕*n.* 職業
(C) attachment〔ə'tætʃmənt〕*n.* 附件
(D) machinery〔mə'ʃinərɪ〕*n.* 機器
memory〔'mɛmərɪ〕*n.* 記憶　　increase〔ɪn'kris〕*v.* 增加
store〔stor〕*v.* 儲存

二、綜合測驗：

　　Kizhi is an island on Lake Onega in Karelia, Russia, with a beautiful collection of wooden churches and houses. It is one of the most popular tourist <u>attractions</u> in Russia and a United Nations Educational, Scientific,
　　　　　　16
and Cultural Organization (UNESCO) World Heritage Site.
　　基日島是一個小島，位在俄羅斯卡累利阿共和國的奧涅加湖，有大量的美麗木造教堂和房屋，是俄羅斯最受歡迎的觀光景點之一，也是聯合國教育科學暨文化組織的世界遺產地點。

island〔'aɪlənd〕*n.* 島嶼　　Russia〔'rʌʃə〕*n.* 俄羅斯
a collection of 大量的　　wooden〔'wʊdn̩〕*adj.* 木製的
popular〔'pɑpjələ〕*adj.* 受歡迎的　　tourist〔'tʊrɪst〕*adj.* 觀光的
United Nations Educational, Scientific, and Cultural Organization
　　聯合國教育科學暨文化組織（ = *UNESCO* ）
heritage〔'hɛrətɪdʒ〕*n.* 遺產　　site〔saɪt〕*n.* 地點
World Heritage Site 世界遺產地點

16. (**D**)　(A) affair〔ə'fɛr〕*n.* 事情；事件
　　　　　(B) fashion〔'fæʃən〕*n.* 流行
　　　　　(C) industry〔'ɪndəstrɪ〕*n.* 工業　　*tourist industry* 旅遊業
　　　　　(D) *attraction*〔ə'trækʃən〕*n.* 吸引力；具吸引力的事物
　　　　　　　tourist attraction 觀光景點

　　The island is about 7 km long and 0.5 km wide. It is surrounded by about 5,000 other islands, some of <u>which</u> are just rocks sticking out of the ground.
　　　　　　　　　　　　　　　　　17
　　這座島大約七公里長，半公里寬，被大約五千座其他島嶼所圍繞，其中有一些只是從地面突出的岩塊。

surround〔sə'raʊnd〕*v.* 圍繞　　rock〔rɑk〕*n.* 岩石
stick〔stɪk〕*v.* 伸出；突出　　*stick out of* 從～突出

17. (**D**)　這裡需填上關係代名詞，來引導形容詞子句，用以修飾先行詞
　　　islands，故選 (D) which。而 (B) that 雖也是關係代名詞，但因之前
　　　有介系詞 of，故不能選；(A) 與 (C) 爲代名詞，不能用以連接形容詞
　　　子句，文法不合。

The entire island of Kizhi is, <u>in fact</u>, an outdoor museum of wooden
　　　　　　　　　　　　　　　　18
architecture created in 1966.　It contains many historically significant and

beautiful wooden structures, <u>including</u> windmills, boathouses, chapels, fish
　　　　　　　　　　　　　　　　19

houses, and homes.

　　事實上，整座基日島就是一座戶外博物館，擁有 1966 年建造的木造建築，
包含許多史上重要的美麗木造建築，包括風車、船屋、教堂、漁屋和房舍等。

　　　　entire〔 ɪn'taɪr 〕*adj.* 整個的　　outdoor〔'aʊt,dor 〕*adj.* 戶外的
　　　　museum〔 mju'ziəm 〕*n.* 博物館
　　　　architecture〔'ɑrkə,tɛktʃɚ 〕*n.* 建築　　contain〔 kən'ten 〕*v.* 包含
　　　　historically〔 hɪs'tɔrɪkl̩ɪ 〕*adv.* 歷史上地
　　　　significant〔 sɪg'nɪfəkənt 〕*adj.* 重要的
　　　　windmill〔'wɪnd,mɪl 〕*n.* 風車　　boathouse〔'bot,haʊs 〕*n.* 船屋
　　　　chapel〔'tʃæpl̩ 〕*n.* 教堂　　　***fish house*** 漁屋

18. (**A**)　(A) ***in fact*** 事實上　　　　　(B) once again　再一次
　　　　　　　(C) as usual　如往常般　　　　(D) for instance　例如

19. (**C**)　(A) except〔 ɪk'sɛpt 〕*prep.* 除…之外（不包括…在內）
　　　　　　　(B) besides〔 bɪ'saɪdz 〕*prep.* 除…之外（包括…在內）
　　　　　　　(C) ***including***〔 ɪn'kludɪŋ 〕*prep.* 包括（= *inclusive of*）
　　　　　　　(D) regarding〔 rɪ'gɑrdɪŋ 〕*prep.* 關於…

The jewel of the architecture is the 22-domed Transfiguration Church, built
in the early 1700s.　It is about 37 m tall, <u>making</u> it one of the tallest log
　　　　　　　　　　　　　　　　　　　　　　　　　20
structures in the world.　The church was built with pine trees brought from
the mainland, which was quite common for the 18th century.

建築之最是擁有 22 個圓頂的「變容教堂」，建造於十八世紀初期，大約 37 公尺
的高度讓它成爲全世界最高的圓木建築之一，它是用歐洲大陸搬來的松木所建
造而成，這樣的情況在十八世紀相當常見。

jewel〔'dʒuəl〕*n.* 珠寶；最有價值的人（物）　　dome〔dom〕*n.* 圓頂
transfiguration〔ˌtrænsfɪgjə'reʃən〕*n.* 變形；改變容貌
log〔lɔg , lɑg〕*n.* 原木；圓木　　pine〔paɪn〕*n.* 松木
mainland〔'menˌlænd , 'menlənd〕*n.* 大陸

20. (**B**) 此處原爲 which makes，因爲省略關代 which，之後的一般動詞須改
　　　爲現在分詞，故選 (B) *making*。

　　There was once a time when all human beings were gods. However,
they often took their divinity for granted and <u>even</u> abused it. Seeing this,
　　　　　　　　　　　　　　　　　　　　　　　21
Brahma, the chief god, decided to take their divinity away from them and
hide it <u>where</u> it could never be found.
　　　22

　　人類曾經一度都是神，然而，他們經常將自己的神性視爲理所當然，甚至
濫用它。衆神之王梵天看了這樣的情形後，決定從他們身上取走神性，並將它
藏在永遠無法找到的地方。

once〔wʌns〕*adv.* 曾經；一度　　*human being* 人類；人
take…for granted 視…爲理所當然
divinity〔də'vɪnətɪ〕*n.* 神性；神的特質
abuse〔ə'bjuz〕*v.* 濫用
Brahma〔'brɑmə〕*n.* （印度敎主神）梵天
chief〔tʃif〕*adj.* 主要的

21. (**B**) 依句意，講到當時人類將具有神的特質視爲理所當然，「甚至」濫用
　　　它，故本題選 (B) *even*〔'ivən〕*adv.* 甚至。
　　　(A) yet〔jɛt〕*adv.* 尙未；然而
　　　(C) never〔'nɛvɚ〕*adv.* 從未
　　　(D) rather〔'ræðɚ〕*adv.* 相當；頗；反之

22. (**C**) 依句意，這裡需塡上表示「在…地方」的連接詞 *where*，來引導後面
　　　的子句，而 (A)「雖然」是表讓步的連接詞；(B)「因爲」是表因果關係
　　　的連接詞；(D)「當…的時候」是表時間的連接詞，皆與文意不合。

　　Brahma called a council of the gods to help him decide on a place to
hide the divinity. The gods suggested that they hide it <u>deep</u> in the earth or
　　　　　　　　　　　　　　　　　　　　　　　　　　　　　　　23

take it to the top of the highest mountain. But Brahma thought <u>neither</u>
24
would do because he believed humans would dig into the earth and climb
every mountain, and eventually find it. So, the gods gave up.

梵天召開眾神會議，來幫祂決定一個地方來藏妥神性。眾神建議將它藏在地底深處，或將它帶至最高的山頂上。但是梵天認為兩者皆不可行，因為他相信人類會挖掘土地，並攀登每一座山，而終究會找到它。於是眾神放棄了。

call〔kɔl〕v. 召喚　　council〔'kaunsḷ〕n. 會議
suggest〔sə'dʒɛst〕v. 建議　　earth〔ɝθ〕n. 土地；地球
human〔'hjumən〕n. 人類；人 (= *human being*)
dig〔dɪg〕v. 挖掘　　eventually〔ɪ'vɛntʃuəlɪ〕adv. 終究；最後
give up 放棄

23. (**C**) 依句意，「將它藏在地底深處」，應選 (C) ***deep***〔dip〕adv. 深深地。
　　(A) close〔klos〕adv. 緊密地；靠近地
　　(B) apart〔ə'part〕adv. 分開地
　　(D) hard〔hard〕adv. 努力地

24. (**D**) 此處依句意，須選擇「兩者皆不」，應用 ***neither***，故本題選 (D)。
　　(A) 每一者；(B) 更多者；(C) 任一者，均不合。

Brahma thought for a long time and finally decided to hide their
divinity in the center of their own being, for humans would never think to
<u>look for</u> it there. Since that time humans have been going up and down the
25
earth, digging, climbing, and exploring—searching for something already
within themselves.

梵天想了很久，最後決定將神性藏在人類的內心深處，因為人們永遠想不到要到那裡尋找。從那時起，人類就一直在地球上到處挖掘、攀登、探尋——尋找那個已經存在他們內心的事物。

being〔'biɪŋ〕n. 存在；生命　　explore〔ɪk'splor〕v. 探索
up and down 到處　　***search for*** 尋找

25. (**A**) (A) ***look for*** 尋找　　(B) get over 克服
　　(C) do without 沒有…也行　　(D) bump into 撞上；偶遇

In the fall of 1973, in an effort to bring attention to the conflict between Egypt and Israel, *World Hello Day* was born. The objective is to promote peace all over the world, and to <u>break down</u> barriers between every
26
nationality. Since then, *World Hello Day*—November 21st of every year—<u>has been</u> observed by people in 180 countries.
27

在 1973 年秋天，爲了讓埃及與以色列的衝突受到關注，「世界你好日」誕生了。目標是爲了促進世界和平，打破各國間的藩籬。從那時起，「世界你好日」——每年的十一月二十一日——就有一百八十個國家的人在過。

> ***in an effort to** + V.* 努力要～；爲了要～
> attention〔ə'tɛnʃən〕 *n.* 注意力　　conflict〔'kɑnflɪkt〕 *n.* 衝突
> Egypt〔'idʒɪpt〕 *n.* 埃及　　Israel〔'ɪzrɪəl〕 *n.* 以色列
> ***World Hello Day*** 世界你好日　　objective〔əb'dʒɛktɪv〕 *n.* 目標
> promote〔prə'mot〕 *v.* 促進；提倡　　peace〔pis〕 *n.* 和平
> barrier〔'bærɪɚ〕 *n.* 藩籬；障礙
> nationality〔,næʃən'ælətɪ〕 *n.* 國籍；國家
> observe〔əb'zɝv〕 *v.* 過（節）

26. (**D**) (A) skip over 略過；跳過　(B) come across 偶遇
　　(C) look into 調查　　　　　(D) ***break down*** 打破；拆除；克服

27. (**B**) 從本句一開始的 since then「從那時起」，可以得知過世界你好日是從過去一直持續到現在，應該用「現在完成式」，故選 (B) ***has been***。

Taking part couldn't be <u>easier</u>. All one has to do is say hello to 10 people
28
on the day. However, in response to the <u>aim</u> of this event, the concepts of
29
fostering peace and harmony do not have to be confined to one day a year.

參加這個活動非常容易，你只要在當天跟十個人問好。然而，爲響應這個活動的目標，促進和平和和諧的觀念不必被侷限在一年中的一天。

> ***take part*** 參加　　***all** sb. **has to do is** + V* 某人所要做的是～
> response〔rɪ'spɑns〕 *n.* 回應；反應　　***in response to*** 爲響應
> event〔ɪ'vɛnt〕 *n.* 事件；活動　　concept〔'kɑnsɛpt〕 *n.* 觀念
> foster〔'fɔstɚ〕 *v.* 培養；促進　　harmony〔'hɑrmənɪ〕 *n.* 和諧
> confine〔kən'faɪn〕 *v.* 限制

28. (**C**) 「cannot/couldn't be + 形容詞比較級」表示「非常…；再…不過」，
依據文意，應選 (C) *easier*，表示「再容易不過；非常容易」的意思。

29. (**A**) 依句意，「爲響應本活動的目標」，應選 (A) *aim*〔 em 〕*n.* 目標。
(B) tone〔 ton 〕*n.* 語調；音調
(C) key〔 ki 〕*n.* 鑰匙；關鍵；祕訣
(D) peak〔 pik 〕*n.* 山峰；尖峰

We can <u>keep</u> the spirit going by communicating often and consciously. It is
　　　30
a simple act that anyone can do and it reminds us that communication is
more effective than conflict.
我們可以藉由經常且有意識地溝通，來讓這樣的精神持續下去，這是一個任何
人都能做的簡單行爲，而且提醒我們，溝通比衝突更有效。

　　　spirit〔'spɪrɪt 〕*n.* 精神　　communicate〔 kə'mjunə,ket 〕*v.* 溝通
　　　consciously〔'kɑnʃəslɪ 〕*adv.* 有意識地
　　　simple〔'sɪmpḷ 〕*adj.* 簡單的　　act〔 ækt 〕*n.* 行爲
　　　remind〔 rɪ'maɪnd 〕*v.* 提醒　　effective〔 ɪ'fɛktɪv 〕*adj.* 有效的

30. (**B**) "keep + O. + V-ing" 表示「使~繼續下去」之意，故選 (B) *keep*。
(A) push〔 puʃ 〕*v.* 推擠　　　　(C) bring〔 brɪŋ 〕*v.* 帶來
(D) make〔 mek 〕*v.* 使得

三、文意選填：

　　Generally there are two ways to name typhoons: the number-based
convention and the list-based convention. Following the number-based
convention, typhoons are coded with [31](I) various types of numbers such as
a 4-digit or a 6-digit code. For example, the 14th typhoon in 2003 can be
labeled either as Typhoon 0314 or Typhoon 200314. The [32](C) disadvantage
of this convention, however, is that a number is hard to remember. The
list-based convention, on the other hand, is based on the list of typhoon
names compiled in advance by a committee, and is more widely used.

　　颱風命名的方式一般有兩種：以編號命名和以命名表命名。按照編號命名
的慣例，颱風會被編上不同種類的編號，像四位數或六位數。例如，2003 年第
十四個颱風，可能被稱爲 0314 號颱風或是 200314 號颱風。然而，這種慣例的
缺點是數字很難記。另一方面，根據一個委員會事先制定的命名表來命名的方
式，則比較廣泛被使用。

generally〔'dʒɛnərəlɪ〕*adv.* 一般地；通常　　name〔nem〕*v.* 命名
typhoon〔taɪ'fun〕*n.* 颱風
convention〔kən'vɛnʃən〕*n.* 習俗；慣例；常規
follow〔'falo〕*v.* 遵照；按照
code〔kod〕*v.* 把…編上編號　*n.* 編號
various〔'vɛrɪəs〕*adj.* 各種不同的
digit〔'dɪdʒɪt〕*n.*（各個）阿拉伯數字
label〔'lebḷ〕*v.* 把…分類（爲）；稱（爲）
either A as B 不是 A 就是 B　　disadvantage〔ˌdɪsəd'væntɪdʒ〕*n.* 缺點
on the other hand 另一方面
compile〔kəm'paɪl〕*v.* 編輯　　***in advance*** 事先；預先
committee〔kə'mɪtɪ〕*n.* 委員會　　widely〔'waɪdlɪ〕*adv.* 廣泛地

At the very beginning, only [33](J) female names were used because at that time typhoons were named after girlfriends or wives of the experts on the committee. In 1979, however, male names were also included because women protested against the original naming [34](F) practice for reasons of gender equality.

　　一開始只有女性的名字被使用，因爲那時候颱風都以委員會裡專家的女朋友或妻子的名字命名。然而，在 1979 年，男性的名字也包含在內，因爲女性以性別平等爲由，抗議原來的命名慣例。

female〔'fimel〕*adj.* 女性的　　***be named after*** 以…的名字命名
expert〔'ɛkspɜt〕*n.* 專家　　male〔mel〕*adj.* 男性的
include〔ɪn'klud〕*v.* 包含　　protest〔prə'tɛst〕*v.* 抗議
original〔ə'rɪdʒənḷ〕*adj.* 原本的；最初的
practice〔'præktɪs〕*n.* 慣例　　reason〔'rizn̩〕*n.* 理由
gender〔'dʒɛndɚ〕*n.* 性別　　equality〔ɪ'kwɑlətɪ〕*n.* 平等

In Asia, Western names were used until 2000 when the committee decided to use Asian names to [35](H) raise Asians' awareness of typhoons. The names were chosen from a name pool [36](D) composed of 140 names, 10 each from the 14 members of the committee. Each country has its unique naming preferences. Korea and Japan [37](B) favor animal names and China likes names of gods such as Longwang (dragon king) and Fengshen (god of the wind).

亞洲一直都使用西方名字爲颱風命名，直到 2000 年，委員會決定使用亞洲名字，以提高亞洲人對颱風的意識。颱風的名字由命名表中選出，這份命名表是由一百四十個名字組成，十四個會員國各提供十個名字。每個國家都有自己獨特的命名喜好。韓國和日本偏好動物名稱，而中國喜歡神的名字，例如「龍王」和「風神」。

Asia〔'eʒə〕*n.* 亞洲　　　raise〔rez〕*v.* 提高
awareness〔ə'wɛrnɪs〕*n.* 意識　　pool〔pul〕*n.* 集合
be composed of 由…組成　　member〔'mɛmbɚ〕*n.* 會員
unique〔ju'nik〕*adj.* 獨特的　　preference〔'prɛfrəns〕*n.* 偏好
favor〔'fevɚ〕*v.* 偏好　　　dragon〔'drægən〕*n.* 龍

After the 140 names are all used in order, they will be [38](E) recycled. But the names can be changed. If a member country suffers great damage from a certain typhoon, it can [39](A) request that the name of the typhoon be deleted from the list at the annual committee meeting. For example, the names of Nabi by South Korea, and Longwang by China were [40](G) replaced with other names in 2007. The deletion of both names was due to the severe damage caused by the typhoons bearing the names.

一百四十個名字都依序使用過後，還會被重新循環使用。但名字是可以改變的。如果颱風在某個委員國造成嚴重損害，該國可以在年度委員會會議上，要求將其除名。例如，由南韓命名的娜比颱風，由中國命名的龍王颱風，在 2007 年皆被以其他的名稱取代。兩者的除名都是由於名叫娜比和龍王的颱風所造成的嚴重損害。

in order 依照順序　　recycle〔ri'saɪk!〕*v.* 循環使用
suffer〔'sʌfɚ〕*v.* 遭受　　damage〔'dæmɪdʒ〕*n.* 損害；破壞
certain〔'sɝtn̩〕*adj.* 某個　　request〔rɪ'kwɛst〕*v.* 要求
delete〔dɪ'lit〕*v.* 刪除　　annual〔'ænjuəl〕*adj.* 年度的
replace〔rɪ'ples〕*v.* 取代　　deletion〔dɪ'liʃən〕*n.* 刪除
be due to 是由於　　severe〔sə'vɪr〕*adj.* 嚴重的
cause〔kɔz〕*v.* 引起；造成　　bear〔bɛr〕*v.* 擁有；帶有

四、閱讀測驗：

41-44 爲題組

The kilt is a skirt traditionally worn by Scottish men. It is a tailored garment that is wrapped around the wearer's body at the waist starting from one side, around the front and back and across the front again to the opposite side. The overlapping layers in front are called "aprons." Usually, the kilt covers the body from the waist down to just above the knees. A properly made kilt should not be so loose that the wearer can easily twist the kilt around the body, nor should it be so tight that it causes bulging of the fabric where it is buckled. Underwear may be worn as one prefers.

　　蘇格蘭裙是一種傳統上由蘇格蘭男士所穿著的裙子。它是一種訂製服，包覆著穿著者的腰際，從一側繞過前面到後面，再繞過前面到另一側。前面重疊的兩層被稱爲「圍裙」。通常，蘇格蘭裙遮蓋腰線以下到正好膝蓋上方的位置。一條以正確方式製作的蘇格蘭裙，不應該寬鬆到穿著者能夠輕易轉動，而也不應該緊到在裙子扣緊的地方造成鼓起的情形。裡面的內衣褲則可以依個人偏好來穿著。

kilt〔kɪlt〕*n.* 蘇格蘭裙　　traditionally〔trəˋdɪʃənlɪ〕*adv.* 傳統地
Scottish〔ˋskɑtɪʃ〕*adj.* 蘇格蘭的　　tailor〔ˋtelɚ〕*v.* 縫製
garment〔ˋgɑrmənt〕*n.* 衣服　　wrap〔ræp〕*v.* 包裹；圍繞
waist〔west〕*n.* 腰　　opposite〔ˋɑpəzɪt〕*adj.* 相反的
overlap〔͵ovɚˋlæp〕*v.* 重疊　　layer〔ˋleɚ〕*n.* 一層
apron〔ˋeprən〕*n.* 圍裙　　cover〔ˋkʌvɚ〕*v.* 遮蓋
knee〔ni〕*n.* 膝蓋　　properly〔ˋprɑpɚlɪ〕*adv.* 適當地；正確地
loose〔lus〕*adj.* 寬鬆的　　twist〔twɪst〕*v.* 纏繞；扭轉
tight〔taɪt〕*adj.* 緊的　　bulge〔bʌldʒ〕*v.* 鼓起
fabric〔ˋfæbrɪk〕*n.* 織品；布料　　buckle〔ˋbʌkḷ〕*v.* 用扣環扣住
underwear〔ˋʌndɚ͵wɛr〕*n.* 內衣褲　　prefer〔prɪˋfɝ〕*v.* 較喜歡

One of the most distinctive features of the kilt is the pattern of squares, or sett, it exhibits. The association of particular patterns with individual families can be traced back hundreds of years. Then in the Victorian era (19th century), weaving companies began to systematically record and formalize the system of setts for commercial purposes. Today there are also setts for States and Provinces, schools and universities, and general patterns that anybody can wear.

　　蘇格蘭裙最獨特的特點之一就是它所展示的方格花紋。特定的花紋和個別家族的關聯可以回溯到數百年前。在維多利亞時期（十九世紀）時，編織公司爲了商業用途，開始有系統地記錄這些樣式，並且使其形式化。今日有各種代表不同州、省份、學校和大學的花紋，還有任何人都可以穿著的一般圖案。

distinctive〔dɪ'stɪŋktɪv〕*adj.* 獨特的　　feature〔'fitʃɚ〕*n.* 特點
pattern〔'pætən〕*n.* 花樣；圖案　　square〔skwɛr〕*n.* 正方形
sett〔sɛt〕*n.* 河床四角形的鋪石；此指蘇格蘭裙的「方格花紋」
exhibit〔ɪg'zɪbɪt〕*v.* 展示　　association〔ə,soʃɪ'eʃən〕*n.* 關聯
particular〔pɚ'tɪkjəlɚ〕*adj.* 特定的
individual〔,ɪndə'vɪdʒuəl〕*adj.* 個別的　　trace〔tres〕*v.* 回溯
Victorian〔vɪk'torɪən〕*adj.* 維多利亞時期的
era〔'ɪrə〕*n.* 時代　　weave〔wiv〕*v.* 編織
systematically〔,sɪstə'mætɪklɪ〕*adv.* 有系統地
formalize〔'fɔrml̩,aɪz〕*v.* 使形式化
system〔'sɪstəm〕*n.* 系統　　commercial〔kə'mɝʃəl〕*adj.* 商業的
purpose〔'pɝpəs〕*n.* 目的　　state〔stet〕*n.* 州
province〔'prɑvɪns〕*n.* 省份　　general〔'dʒɛnərəl〕*adj.* 一般的

The kilt can be worn with accessories. On the front apron, there is often a kilt pin, topped with a small decorative family symbol. A small knife can be worn with the kilt too. It typically comes in a very wide variety, from fairly plain to quite elaborate silver- and jewel-ornamented designs. The kilt can also be worn with a sporran, which is the Gaelic word for pouch or purse.

穿著蘇格蘭裙可以搭配配件。在前面的圍裙，通常會有一個裙子的別針，別針上蓋有小型裝飾性的家族象徵。穿蘇格蘭裙也可以配戴小刀，小刀通常有豐富的種類，從相當樸素到頗爲細緻，還搭配銀飾和珠寶設計的都有。蘇格蘭裙也可搭配毛布袋，毛布袋就是蓋爾語裡的囊袋或錢包。

accessory〔æk'sɛsərɪ〕*n.* 配件　　front〔frʌnt〕*adj.* 前面的
pin〔pɪn〕*n.* 大頭針；別針　　top〔tɑp〕*v.* 加蓋
decorative〔'dɛkə,retɪv〕*adj.* 裝飾性的　　symbol〔'sɪmbl̩〕*n.* 象徵
typically〔'tɪpɪklɪ〕*adv.* 典型地；通常　　***come in*** 有～
variety〔və'raɪətɪ〕*n.* 多樣　　fairly〔'fɛrlɪ〕*adv.* 相當地
plain〔plen〕*adj.* 樸素的　　quite〔kwaɪt〕*adv.* 相當地
elaborate〔ɪ'læbərɪt〕*adj.* 精巧的　　jewel〔'dʒuəl〕*n.* 珠寶
ornament〔'ɔrnə,mɛnt〕*v.* 裝飾　　design〔dɪ'zaɪn〕*n.* 設計；圖案
sporran〔'spɔrən〕*n.* 毛布袋　　Gaelic〔'gelɪk〕*adj.* 蓋爾語的
pouch〔pautʃ〕*n.* 囊袋

41. (**D**) 穿著蘇格蘭裙適當的方式爲何？
　　(A) 裡面應該穿著內衣褲。　　(B) 應該夠寬鬆以便旋轉。

(C) 應該長到可以遮住穿著者的膝蓋。

(D) 身體正面應該包覆兩層。

proper〔ˈprɑpɚ〕*adj.* 適當的

underneath〔ˌʌndəˈniθ〕*prep.* 在～之下

42. (**A**) 下列何者是蘇格蘭裙方格花紋的正確描述？

(A) 它們曾經是不同蘇格蘭家族的象徵。

(B) 它們是爲了商業目的而由政府建立的。

(C) 它們在十九世紀時代表不同的州和省份。

(D) 它們曾經有一種普遍的樣式讓所有的人和機構穿著。

description〔dɪˈskrɪpʃən〕*n.* 描述

establish〔əˈstæblɪʃ〕*v.* 建立　　represent〔ˌrɛprɪˈzɛnt〕*v.* 代表

used to V. 曾經　　individual〔ˌɪndəˈvɪdʒuəl〕*n.* 個人

institution〔ˌɪnstəˈtjuʃən〕*n.* 機構

43. (**C**) 下列何者通常不和蘇格蘭裙搭配來當作裝飾？

(A) 別針。　　　　　　　　　(B) 錢包。

(C) 鮮紅色的圍裙。　　　　　(D) 銀刀。

ruby〔ˈrubɪ〕*adj.* 鮮紅色的

44. (**A**) 本文的目的爲何？

(A) 介紹一種蘇格蘭的衣服。　(B) 廣告一種編織的樣式。

(C) 說服男士穿著蘇格蘭裙。　(D) 比較一般的裙子和蘇格蘭裙。

advertise〔ˈædvɚˌtaɪz〕*v.* 廣告

persuade〔pɚˈswed〕*v.* 說服　　compare〔kəmˈpɛr〕*v.* 比較

45-48 爲題組

Wesla Whitfield, a famous jazz singer, has a unique style and life story, so I decided to see one of her performances and interview her for my column.

　　名爵士歌手薇絲拉‧惠特菲爾有著獨特的表演風格，以及特別的人生故事，所以我決定去觀賞一場她的演出，並做訪談，以撰寫我的專欄。

unique〔juˈnik〕*adj.* 獨特的　　style〔staɪl〕*n.* 風格

performance〔pɚˈfɔrməns〕*n.* 表演

interview〔ˈɪntɚˌvju〕*v.* 訪談　　column〔ˈkɑləm〕*n.*（報紙）專欄

I went to a nightclub in New York and watched the stage lights go up. After the band played an introduction, Wesla Whitfield wheeled herself onstage in a wheelchair. As she sang, Whitfield's voice was so powerful and soulful that everyone in the room forgot the wheelchair was even there.

　　我來到紐約的一家夜店，看著舞台燈光亮起。在樂團演奏完序曲後，惠特菲爾自己推著輪椅上舞台。當惠特菲爾開口唱歌時，她的聲音強而有力，而且充滿感情，在場的每個人甚至都忘了輪椅的存在。

> nightclub〔'naɪt͵klʌb〕*n.* 夜店；夜總會　　***go up***　（燈）亮起
> introduction〔͵ɪntrə'dʌkʃən〕*n.* 序曲；序文
> wheel〔hwil〕*v.* 推動（有輪子的東西）
> onstage〔'ɑn'stedʒ〕*adv.* 上舞台　　wheelchair〔'hwil'tʃɛr〕*n.* 輪椅
> soulful〔'solfəl〕*adj.* 充滿感情的

　　At 57, Whitfield is small and pretty, witty and humble, persistent and philosophical. Raised in California, Whitfield began performing in public at age 18, when she took a job as a singing waitress at a pizza parlor. After studying classical music in college, she moved to San Francisco and went on to sing with the San Francisco Opera Chorus.

　　五十七歲的惠特菲爾嬌小可愛，個性詼諧又謙卑，不輕言放棄而且相當豁達。加州長大的惠特菲爾，十八歲時開始在公開場合演出，那時她在披薩店擔任駐唱女服務生。惠特菲爾在大學主修古典音樂，畢業後搬到舊金山，接著就加入舊金山歌劇院合唱團。

> pretty〔'prɪtɪ〕*adj.* 可愛的；漂亮的
> witty〔'wɪtɪ〕*adj.* 機靈的；詼諧的　　humble〔'hʌmbl̩〕*adj.* 謙虛的
> persistent〔pə'zɪstənt〕*adj.* 堅忍不拔的
> philosophical〔͵fɪlə'sɑfɪkl̩〕*adj.* 達觀的；想得開的
> raise〔rez〕*v.* 養育　　***in public***　公開地
> ***singing waitress*** 駐唱女服務生【服務客人並上台演唱的女服務生】
> parlor〔'pɑrlɚ〕*n.*（某種職業的）店鋪
> classical〔'klæsɪkl̩〕*adj.* 古典的　　***go on to V.*** 接著～
> opera〔'ɑpərə〕*n.* 歌劇；歌劇院　　chorus〔'korəs〕*n.* 合唱團
> ***San Francisco Opera Chorus*** 舊金山歌劇院合唱團

　　Walking home from rehearsal at age 29, she was caught in the midst of a random shooting that left her paralyzed from the waist down. I asked how she dealt with the realization that she'd never walk again, and she confessed that initially she didn't want to face it. After a year of depression she tried to kill herself. She was then admitted to a hospital for treatment, where she was able to recover.

　　二十九歲那年，當她排練結束，走路回家的路上，遇到有人隨意開槍掃射，被流彈波及，使她從此腰部以下癱瘓。我問她知道自己再也不能走路時，她如何應付，她坦承一開始她無法面對。憂鬱了一年後，她企圖自殺，然後就被送到醫院治療，並在醫院康復。

> rehearsal〔rɪ'hɝsl̩〕*n.*（戲劇等）排演
> ***be caught in*** 遇到（不好的情況）
> ***in the midst of*** 在…進行之中（ *= in the middle of* ）
> random〔'rændəm〕*adj.* 漫無目的的；隨便的
> ***random shooting*** （無特定目標的）亂槍掃射
> paralyze〔'pærə,laɪz〕*v.* 使癱瘓　　　waist〔west〕*n.* 腰部
> ***deal with*** 處理；應付　　realization〔,rɪələ'zeʃən〕*n.* 認識；了解
> confess〔kən'fɛs〕*v.* 坦承　　initially〔ɪ'nɪʃəlɪ〕*adv.* 最初
> depression〔dɪ'prɛʃən〕*n.* 憂鬱　***kill* oneself** 自殺
> admit〔əd'mɪt〕*v.* 送去（醫院）　　treatment〔'tritmənt〕*n.* 治療
> recover〔rɪ'kʌvɚ〕*v.* 恢復

　　Whitfield said she came to understand that the only thing she had lost in this misfortunate event was the ability to walk. She still possessed her most valuable asset—her mind. Pointing to her head, she said, "Everything important is in here. The only real disability in life is losing your mind." When I asked if she was angry about what she had lost, she admitted to being frustrated occasionally, "especially when everybody's dancing, because I love to dance. But **when that happens** I just remove myself so I can focus instead on what I can do."

　　惠特菲爾說她後來了解到，在這場不幸的意外中，她唯一失去的東西就是行走的能力。她仍然擁有最有價值的資產——她的心智。她指著頭說：「重要的東西都裝在這兒。人生中唯一真正的殘障就是喪志。」當我問到她對已經失去的東西生不生氣時，她承認偶爾會感到沮喪，「尤其是當每個人都在跳舞的時候，因為我喜歡跳舞。但在那樣的情況下，我通常會離開現場，這樣我才能專注在我能做的事情上。」

> misfortunate〔mɪs'fɔrtʃənɪt〕*adj.* 不幸的　　event〔ɪ'vɛnt〕*n.* 事件
> ability〔ə'bɪlətɪ〕*n.* 能力　　possess〔pə'zɛs〕*v.* 擁有
> valuable〔'væljəbl̩〕*adj.* 有價值的　　asset〔'æsɛt〕*n.* 資產
> disability〔,dɪsə'bɪlətɪ〕*n.* 殘疾　　admit〔əd'mɪt〕*v.* 承認
> frustrated〔'frʌstretɪd〕*adj.* 受挫的
> occassionally〔ə'keʒənlɪ〕*adv.* 偶爾　　remove〔rɪ'muv〕*v.* 移除
> ***remove* oneself** 走開；離去　　***focus on*** 專注於
> instead〔ɪn'stɛd〕*adv.* 作為代替

45. (**C**) 薇絲拉‧惠特菲爾曾在下列何處工作過？
　　(A) 大學。　　　　　　　　(B) 醫院。
　　(C) 披薩店。　　　　　　　(D) 通訊社。
　　news agency 通訊社

46. (**D**) 最後一段的「在那樣的情況下」指的是什麼？
　　(A) 薇絲拉喪志時。　　　　(B) 薇絲拉在台上演唱時。
　　(C) 薇絲拉坐輪椅出門時。　(D) 薇絲拉在看其他人跳舞時。

47. (**B**) 以下對薇絲拉‧惠特菲爾殘疾的敘述何者為真？
　　(A) 她的殘疾是由交通意外所引起。
　　(B) 一開始她很傷心而且沮喪。
　　(C) 她的殘疾嚴重影響她的唱歌生涯。
　　(D) 這是她在大學時發生的事。
　　physical〔ˈfɪzɪk!〕*adj.* 身體上的　　depressed〔dɪˈprɛst〕*adj.* 沮喪的

48. (**A**) 薇絲拉最有可能給其他殘障人士什麼建議？
　　(A) 不要理會你已經失去的，要充分利用你所擁有的。
　　(B) 要謙虛，而且努力以贏得他人的尊敬。
　　(C) 學習一項技術，你仍然可以成功成名。
　　(D) 每當覺得不高興或沮喪時，試著唱唱歌。
　　advice〔ədˈvaɪs〕*n.* 忠告；建議　　disabled〔dɪsˈeb!d〕*adj.* 殘障的
　　ignore〔ɪgˈnor〕*v.* 忽視；不理　　***make the best use of*** 善加利用
　　modest〔ˈmɑdɪst〕*adj.* 謙虛的　　earn〔ɝn〕*v.* 贏得
　　acquire〔əˈkwaɪr〕*v.* 獲得；學得　　upset〔ʌpˈsɛt〕*adj.* 不高興的

49-52 為題組

　　Forks trace their origins back to the ancient Greeks. Forks at that time were fairly large with two tines that aided in the carving of meat in the kitchen. The tines prevented meat from twisting or moving during carving and allowed food to slide off more easily than it would with a knife.

　　叉子的的起源可以追溯到古希臘人。當時的叉子很大，有兩條叉齒可在廚房用來協助切肉。叉齒可以在切肉時，固定肉不讓它扭動或移動，和用刀子比起來，也可以讓食物較容易滑落。

　　　　fork〔fɔrk〕*n.* 叉子　　trace〔tres〕*v.* 追溯
　　　　origin〔ˈɔrədʒɪn〕*n.* 起源

ancient (ˈenʃənt) *adj.* 古代的   Greek (grik) *n.* 希臘人

fairly (ˈfɛrlɪ) *adv.* 相當   tine (taɪn) *n.* 叉；尖齒

aid (ed) *v.* 幫助   carve (kɑrv) *v.* 切

prevent~from··· 使~不會···   twist (twɪst) *v.* 扭曲

move (muv) *v.* 移動   slide (slaɪd) *v.* 滑

By the 7th century A.D., royal courts of the Middle East began to use forks at the table for dining. From the 10th through the 13th centuries, forks were fairly common among the wealthy in Byzantium. In the 11th century, a Byzantine wife brought forks to Italy; however, they were not widely adopted there until the 16th century. Then in 1533, forks were brought from Italy to France. The French were also slow to accept forks, for using them was thought to be awkward.

到了西元七世紀，中東的皇室開始在餐桌上使用叉子用餐。從十世紀到十三世紀，在拜占庭的富人中，叉子的使用很普遍。在十一世紀，有一位拜占庭的婦人把叉子帶到義大利，然而，一直到十六世紀，叉子在那裡才被廣泛使用。之後，在1533年，叉子從義大利被帶到法國，法國人也是很慢才接受叉子，因為使用叉子被認為很笨拙。

A.D. 西元···年【拉丁文 Anno Domini，表示 in the year of our lord，原意為「主的紀年」】   royal (ˈrɔɪəl) *adj.* 王室的

court (kort) *n.* 宮廷   ***the Middle East*** 中東【中東位於東西半球之間，地跨赤道南北，是亞洲與非洲相連接的地區。中東涵蓋阿拉伯半島及波斯灣區，東接土庫曼、阿富汗及巴基斯坦，南瀕阿拉伯海及印度洋，西臨波斯灣、埃及和地中海，北至黑海及大高加索山脈與歐洲相隔。】

common (ˈkɑmən) *adj.* 普遍的   ***the wealthy*** 富人

Byzantium (bɪˈzæntɪəm) *n.* 拜占庭【古羅馬城市，今稱伊斯坦堡】

Byzantine (bɪˈzɛntɪn) *adj.* 拜占庭的

Italy (ˈɪtḷɪ) *n.* 義大利   widely (ˈwaɪdlɪ) *adv.* 廣泛地

adopt (əˈdɑpt) *v.* 採用   France (fræns) *n.* 法國

the French 法國人   awkward (ˈɔkwəd) *adj.* 笨拙的

In 1608, forks were brought to England by Thomas Coryate, who saw them during his travels in Italy. The English first ridiculed forks as being unnecessary. "Why should a person need a fork when God had given him hands?" they asked. Slowly, however, forks came to be adopted by the wealthy as a symbol of their social status.　They were prized possessions made of expensive materials intended to impress guests.　By the mid 1600s, eating with forks was considered fashionable among the wealthy British.

　　在1608年，叉子被湯姆斯・柯里亞特帶到英國，他是在義大利旅遊時看到叉子的。英國人一開始嘲笑叉子，覺得沒有必要。「當上帝已經賦予人雙手，人爲什麼要用叉子？」然而，慢慢地，叉子開始被有錢人使用，作爲他們社會地位的象徵。叉子是有價值的財產，是用昂貴的材料製成，要用來讓客人留下深刻印象。到了十七世紀中期，在有錢的英國人眼中，用叉子吃東西被視爲是很時尚的行爲。

ridicule〔'rɪdɪ͵kjul〕*v.* 嘲笑
unnecessary〔ʌn'nɛsə͵sɛrɪ〕*adj.* 不必要的
come to + V. 開始⋯　　symbol〔'sɪmbḷ〕*n.* 象徵
status〔'stetəs , 'stætəs〕*n.* 地位　　***social status*** 社會地位
prized〔praɪzd〕*adj.* 非常有價值的；珍貴的
possessions〔pə'zɛʃənz〕*n. pl.* 財產；所有物
be made of 由⋯製成　　material〔mə'tɪrɪəl〕*n.* 物質；材料
intend〔ɪn'tɛnd〕*v.* 打算
be intended to + V. 目的是爲了⋯
impress〔ɪm'prɛs〕*v.* 使印象深刻　　mid〔mɪd〕*adj.* 中間的
fashionable〔'fæʃənəbḷ〕*adj.* 流行的　　***the British*** 英國人

Early table forks were modeled after kitchen forks, but small pieces of food often fell through the two tines or slipped off easily.　In late 17th century France, larger forks with four curved tines were developed.　The additional tines made diners less likely to drop food, and the curved tines served as a scoop so people did not have to constantly switch to a spoon while eating.　By the early 19th century, four-tined forks had also been developed in Germany and England and slowly began to spread to America.

　　早期餐桌上用的叉子是仿造廚房的叉子做成的，但是小塊的食物會從兩齒中掉出，或是容易滑落。在十七世紀晚期的法國，較大的叉子，並帶有四支彎曲的叉齒研發出來；額外的叉齒讓用餐者較不會掉食物，而彎曲的叉齒也可充當杓子，如此一來，人們就不用一直在吃飯的時候改換用湯匙。到十九世紀早期，四齒叉子也在德國和英國發展出來，並開始慢慢擴及到美國。

model〔'madl〕*v.* 製作；仿製 < *after* >　　slip〔slɪp〕*v.* 滑落
curved〔kɜvd〕*adj.* 彎曲的　　develop〔dɪ'vɛləp〕*v.* 發展；研發
additional〔ə'dɪʃənl〕*adj.* 額外的　　diner〔'daɪnɚ〕*n.* 用餐的人
serve as 充當　　scoop〔skup〕*n.* 杓子　*v.* 舀取
constantly〔'kɑnstəntlɪ〕*adv.* 不斷地
switch〔swɪtʃ〕*v.* 轉換　　spread〔sprɛd〕*v.* 傳播

49.(**C**) 這篇文章的主旨爲何？
　　(A) 不同叉子的設計。　　　　　(B) 有叉子協助烹飪的擴張。
　　(C) <u>使用叉子用餐的歷史。</u>　　(D) 有關叉子的餐桌禮儀發展。
　　table manners 餐桌禮儀

50.(**B**) 叉子的使用是透過什麼路線發展？
　　(A) 中東→希臘→英國→義大利→法國。
　　(B) <u>希臘→中東→義大利→法國→英國。</u>
　　(C) 希臘→中東→法國→義大利→德國。
　　(D) 中東→法國→英國→義大利→德國。
　　route〔rut〕*n.* 路線

51.(**D**) 叉子是如何在英國變熱門？
　　(A) 有錢的英國人對叉子的設計印象深刻。
　　(B) 有錢的英國人認爲用手吃飯很笨拙。
　　(C) 有錢的英國人送特別的叉子給貴族作爲奢侈的禮物。
　　(D) <u>有錢的英國人認爲用叉子用餐是社會地位的表徵。</u>
　　noble〔'nobl〕*n.* 貴族（常用複數）
　　luxurious〔lʌg'ʒʊrɪəs〕*adj.* 奢侈的

52.(**A**) 爲什麼叉子要做成彎曲的形狀？
　　(A) <u>它們也可以用來舀取食物。</u>　(B) 這樣看來比較時尚。
　　(C) 這樣設計可以出口給美國。
　　(D) 這樣可以確保在切肉的時候不會扭曲。
　　export〔'ɛksport〕*n.* 出口　　ensure〔ɪn'ʃur〕*v.* 保證

<u>53-56 爲題組</u>

　　Animals are a favorite subject of many photographers. Cats, dogs, and other pets top the list, followed by zoo animals. However, because it's hard to get them to sit still and "perform on command," some professional photographers refuse to photograph pets.

　　動物是許多攝影師最愛的拍攝對象。前幾名是貓、狗以及其它寵物，然後是動物園裡的動物。然而，因爲要讓牠們坐定並且「照命令演出」頗爲困難，有些職業的攝影師拒絕拍攝寵物。

　　　　subject〔'sʌbdʒɪkt〕n. 主題；（照片）被拍攝的物體
　　　　photographer〔fə'tɑgrəfə〕n. 攝影師　　　pet〔pɛt〕n. 寵物
　　　　top〔tɑp〕v. 位於…的頂端　　***top the list*** 位居排行榜的首位
　　　　followed by 接著就是　　　still〔stɪl〕adj. 靜止的；不動的
　　　　sit still 坐著不動　　　perform〔pə'fɔrm〕v. 表演；表現
　　　　command〔kə'mænd〕n. 命令；指揮
　　　　professional〔prə'fɛʃənl〕adj. 職業的
　　　　refuse〔rɪ'fjuz〕v. 拒絕　　　photograph〔'fotə,græf〕v. 拍攝

　　One way to get an appealing portrait of a cat or dog is to hold a biscuit or treat above the camera. The animal's longing look toward the food will be captured by the camera, but the treat won't appear in the picture because it's out of the camera's range. When you show the picture to your friends afterwards, they'll be impressed by your pet's loving expression.

　　想拍出吸引人的貓或狗的照片，方法之一是拿一塊餅乾或小點心在照相機上方。動物看著食物的渴望眼神會被鏡頭捕捉，食物則因爲落在鏡頭範圍之外而不會出現在照片裡。之後當你把照片秀給你的朋友看時，他們會因你的寵物那充滿愛意的眼光而感到印象深刻。

　　　　appealing〔ə'pilɪŋ〕adj. 吸引人的
　　　　portrait〔'portret〕n. 肖像畫；畫像；此指「照片」
　　　　hold〔hold〕v. 握住；拿著　　　biscuit〔'bɪskɪt〕n. 餅乾
　　　　treat〔trit〕n. 美味食物　　　camera〔'kæmərə〕n. 照相機
　　　　longing〔'lɔŋɪŋ〕adj. 渴望的　　　look〔lʊk〕n. 眼神；樣子
　　　　toward〔tord〕prep. 對於　　　capture〔'kæptʃə〕v. 捕捉
　　　　appear〔ə'pɪr〕v. 出現　　　range〔rendʒ〕n. 範圍
　　　　show A to B 把 A 拿給 B 看
　　　　afterwards〔'æftəwədz〕adv. 之後；後來
　　　　impress〔ɪm'prɛs〕v. 使印象深刻
　　　　loving〔'lʌvɪŋ〕adj. 充滿愛的　　　expression〔ɪk'sprɛʃən〕n. 表情

　　If you are using fast film, you can take some good, quick shots of a pet by simply snapping a picture right after calling its name. You'll get a different expression from your pet using this technique. Depending on your pet's mood, the picture will capture an interested, curious expression or possibly a look of annoyance, especially if you've awakened it from a nap.

如果你用的是感光快的底片，只要在叫喚你寵物的名字後馬上拍照，你就能拍出一些又快又好的照片。用這種技巧，你可以拍到寵物不同的表情。視寵物的心情而定，照片可能捕捉到牠們感興趣的、好奇的表情。或者，也可能是感到惱怒的表情，尤其當你吵醒小睡的牠們時。

> film〔fɪlm〕*n.* 底片　　***fast film*** 感光快的底片
> shot〔ʃɑt〕*n.* 照片（= *photograph*）　　***take a shot*** 拍照
> simply〔'sɪmplɪ〕*adv.* 僅僅；只是　　snap〔snæp〕*v.* 喀擦一聲拍（照）
> ***snap a picture*** 快速拍張照片　　technique〔tɛk'nik〕*n.* 技巧
> ***depend on*** 視…而定；取決於　　mood〔mud〕*n.* 心情
> interested〔'ɪntrɪstɪd〕*adj.* 感興趣的　　curious〔'kjʊrɪəs〕*adj.* 好奇的
> annoyance〔ə'nɔɪəns〕*n.* 惱怒
> especially〔ə'spɛʃəlɪ〕*adv.* 尤其；特別是
> awaken〔ə'wekən〕*v.* 叫醒　　nap〔næp〕*n.* 午睡；小睡

Taking pictures of zoo animals requires a little more patience. After all, you can't wake up a lion! You may have to wait for a while until the animal does something interesting or moves into a position for you to get a good shot. When photographing zoo animals, don't get too close to the cages, and never tap on the glass or throw things between the bars of a cage. Concentrate on shooting some good pictures, and always respect the animals you are photographing.

拍攝動物園裡的動物照片需要更多一點的耐性。畢竟，你可不能去驚醒一隻獅子！你可能必須等上一陣子，等那些動物做出一些有趣的事，或是擺出可以讓你拍出好照片的姿勢。在拍攝動物園裡的動物時，不要太靠近籠子、拍打玻璃，或是從鐵籠的間隙丟東西進去。專心拍出好照片，而且永遠要尊敬你正在拍攝的動物。

> require〔rɪ'kwaɪr〕*v.* 需要　　patience〔'peʃəns〕*n.* 耐心
> ***after all*** 畢竟　　***wake up*** 叫醒
> move〔muv〕*v.* 移動；改變姿勢　　position〔pə'zɪʃən〕*n.* 姿勢
> cage〔kedʒ〕*n.* 籠子　　tap〔tæp〕*v.* 輕敲
> bar〔bɑr〕*n.* 金屬條；柵欄
> concentrate〔'kɑnsn̩͵tret〕*v.* 集中；專心　　shoot〔ʃut〕*v.* 拍攝
> respect〔rɪ'spɛkt〕*v.* 尊重

53. (**A**) 為何有些職業攝影師不喜歡拍攝寵物的照片？
　　(A) 寵物可能不會遵守命令。　　(B) 寵物不想被打擾。
　　(C) 寵物可能不喜歡攝影師。　　(D) 寵物很少改變表情。
　　follow〔ˈfɑlo〕*v.* 遵守
　　order〔ˈɔrdɚ〕*n.* 命令　　bother〔ˈbɑðɚ〕*v.* 打擾

54. (**A**) 拍寵物照時，餅乾的作用為何？
　　(A) 捕捉可愛的表情。　　(B) 製造特別的氣氛。
　　(C) 激起寵物的食慾。　　(D) 阻止寵物直視鏡頭。
　　cute〔kjut〕*adj.* 可愛的　　atmosphere〔ˈætməsˌfɪr〕*n.* 氣氛
　　arouse〔əˈrauz〕*v.* 激起　　appetite〔ˈæpəˌtaɪt〕*n.* 食慾
　　keep…from 阻止…

55. (**D**) 拍寵物照時，叫喚寵物的名字有何好處？
　　(A) 幫助你的寵物展現最佳樣貌。
　　(B) 確保你的寵物坐定不動。
　　(C) 讓你的寵物暫時保持清醒。
　　(D) 捕捉你寵物的不同表情。

56. (**D**) 拍攝寵物與拍攝動物園裡的動物，在哪方面不同？
　　(A) 你需要有感光快的底片。　　(B) 你需要特殊設備。
　　(C) 你需要靠近動物。
　　(D) 你需要花更多時間觀望等待。
　　equipment〔ɪˈkwɪpmənt〕*n.* 設備；裝備

第貳部分：非選擇題

一、中譯英

1. 近年來，許多台灣製作的影片已經受到國際的重視。

In recent years, many Taiwan-produced movies have gained international recognition/appreciation.

2. 拍攝這些電影的地點也成為熱門觀光景點。

The places where these movies were filmed have also become popular/hot tourist attractions/spots.

二、英文作文：

Dear Ken,   Jan.18, 2012

You know that I always support you but you've been spending far too much time playing video games—and suffering the consequences as a result. Of course, I love video games too and I understand how easy it is to get wrapped up in them. However, when the games begin to have an effect on your education and relationships, something has to give.

Moderation is the key to everything and video games are no exception. I'm not saying you should stop playing video games altogether but I am strongly suggesting you cut back a little, if for no other reason than to keep your parents off your back. You could try my method, which is to set a limit of two hours per day. I think you'll come to realize that life will be much easier when your parents aren't constantly scolding you. And besides, you really don't want to mess up your future, do you? Anyway, if there's anything I can do to help you, don't hesitate to ask.

Your Friend,
Jack

support〔 sə'port 〕*v.* 支持　　***video game*** 電玩
suffer〔'sʌfɚ 〕*v.* 遭受　　consequence〔'kɑnsə,kwɛns 〕*n.* 後果
as a result 因此　　***be wrapped up in*** 醉心於；迷戀
have an effect on 對…有影響　　education〔,ɛdʒə'keʃən 〕*n.* 教育
relationship〔 rɪ'leʃən,ʃɪp 〕*n.* 關係
moderation〔,mɑdə'reʃən 〕*n.* 適度；節制
key〔 ki 〕*n.* 關鍵　　***be no exception*** ～也不例外
altogether〔,ɔltə'gɛðɚ 〕*adv.* 完全　　***cut back*** 減少
keep *sb.* ***off*** *one's* ***back*** 使某人不嘮叨
method〔'mɛθəd 〕*n.* 方法
constantly〔'kɑnstəntlɪ 〕*adv.* 不斷地　　scold〔 skold 〕*v.* 責罵
mess up 搞砸　　hesitate〔'hɛzə,tet 〕*v.* 猶豫

101 年學測英文科試題修正意見

題　號	題　　　　　目	修　正　意　見
第 8 題	If you fly from Taipei to Tokyo, you'll be taking an international, rather than *a domestic flight.* → … an international, rather than *a* an domestic, *flight.*	an international 和 a domestic 對等，修飾 flight，故須用逗點分隔對比的單字、片語或句子較佳。 【詳見「文法寶典」p.40】
第 9 題	The memory of *the new computer* has …. → The memory of *the computer* …	依句意，應該是原來的電腦擴充記憶體，故須將 new 去掉。
第 16－20 題 第 5 行	…are just rocks sticking out of the *ground.* → … are just rocks sticking out of the *water.*	依句意，島嶼散佈於海上，某些突出於「水面」，故須將 ground 改成 water 較佳。
第 26－30 題 第二段 第 2 行	However, *in response to the* ＿＿29＿＿ *of this event*, the concepts of fostering peace and harmony do not have to be confined to one day a year.… → However, the concepts of fostering peace and harmony do not have to be confined to one day a year.…	in response to 意為「回應；響應」，但此句並沒有回應上句的意思，導致意義上的模糊不清，為多餘的資訊，故應將 in response to the ＿＿29＿＿ of this event 刪除。

題　　號	題　　　目	修　正　意　見
第 31 – 40 題 第三段 第 1 行	In Asia, Western names were used until *2000 when* the committee .... → In Asia, Western names were used until ***2000, when*** the committee	「2000 年」爲補述用法，when 引導的副詞子句前，應有逗點。 【詳見「文法寶典」p.244】
第 41 – 44 題 第二段 第 2 行	*Then in* the Victorian era (19th century) .... → ***In*** the Victorian era (19th century)	上下句並沒有表示時間前後的順序，故應把 Then 去掉。
第 41 – 44 題 第三段 第 2 行	*It* typically *comes* in a very wide variety .... → ***Knives*** typically ***come*** in a very wide variety	爲了避免 It 的指涉模糊，因爲可能指前句說的 knife，也可能指 sett，兩者皆爲單數，故改成 Knives 以避免混淆。
第 41 題 (B)	It should *loosely fit* on the body *to be* turned around. → It should ***fit loosely*** on the body ***so that it can*** be turned around.	loosely 修飾動詞 fit，應放在後方；so that 表示「以便於」，較符合句意。
第 42 題	Which of the following is a correct description *about* setts? → Which of the following is a correct description ***of*** setts?	「description of + N」爲固定用法。

101 年學測英文科考題出題來源

題　　號	出　　　　　　　　　　　　　　處
一、詞彙 第 1～15 題	所有各題對錯答案的選項，均出自「高中常用 7000 字」。
二、綜合測驗 第 16～20 題 第 21～25 題 第 26～30 題	改寫自 Wooden Miracle In Kizhi Island 一文。 改寫自 According to an old Hindu legend... 一文。 改寫自 World Hello Day 一文。
三、文意選填 第 31～40 題	出自 Digital Typhoon: Typhoon Names 一文。
四、閱讀測驗 第 41～44 題 第 45～48 題 第 49～52 題 第 53～56 題	取材自 Kilt 一文。 改編自關於歌手 Wesla Whitfield 的文章。 改寫自 A History of Dining Utensils 一文。 改寫自 Photographing Animals 一文。

【101 年學測】綜合測驗：16-20 出題來源──Blogspot

Wooden Miracle In Kizhi Island

　　Kizhi is an island on Lake Onega in the Republic of Karelia (Medvezhyegorsky District), Russia with a beautiful ensemble of wooden churches, chapels and houses. It is one of the most popular tourist destinations in Russia and a World Heritage Site.

　　The island is about 7 km long and 0.5 km wide. It is surrounded by about 5,000 other islands, most of which are very small. The world famous Kizhi Museum is one of the largest out-door museums in Russia – was founded in 1966.

The museum collections contain 83 pieces of the wooden architecture. The core of the collection is an outstanding sample of the wooden architecture – the architectural ensemble of the Kizhi Pogost of Our Savior built on Kizhi Island in the 18 th and the 19 th centuries. In 1990 the ensemble entered the World Heritage List of UNESCO. In 1993 the Kizhi Museum was entered the List of Cultural Objects of Special Value of the Peoples of the Russian Federation by Order of the President.

More than 150 thousand people visit the museum every year. More than 5 million people have visited the museum so far. The museum has very rich collections of the items connected with the cultural history, which demonstrate the subject environment of the past and reveal interrelations of the cultural traditions of the different peoples living in Karelia.

⋮

【101 年學測】綜合測驗：21-25 出題來源──Naute.com

According to an old Hindu legend…

..there was once a time when all human beings were gods, but they so abused their divinity that Brahma, the chief god, decided to take it away from them and hide it where it could never be found.

Where to hide their divinity was the question. So Brahma called a council of the gods to help him decide. "Let's bury it deep in the earth," said the gods. But Brahma answered, "No, that will not do because humans will dig into the earth and find it." Then the gods said, "Let's sink it in the deepest ocean." But Brahma said, "No, not there, for they will learn to dive into the ocean and will find it." Then the gods said, "Let's take it to the top of the highest mountain and hide it there." But once again Brahma replied, "No, that will not do either, because they will eventually climb every mountain and once again take up their divinity." Then the gods gave up and said, "We do not know where to hide it, because it seems that there is no

place on earth or in the sea that human beings will not eventually reach."
Brahma thought for a long time and then said, "Here is what we will do. We
will hide their divinity deep in the center of their own being, for humans
will never think to look for it there."

All the gods agreed that this was the perfect hiding place, and the deed
was done. And since that time humans have been going up and down the
earth, digging, diving, climbing, and exploring--searching for something
already within themselves.

【101 年學測】文意選填：26-30 出題來源──Wikipedia

World Hello Day

Every year, November 21 is World Hello Day. The objective is to say
hello to ten people on the day. By greeting others, the message is for world
leaders to use communication rather than using force to settle conflicts.
The event began in 1973 by Brian and Michael McCormack in response to
the Yom Kippur War. Since then World Hello Day has been observed by
people in 180 countries.

November 21, 2011 is the 39th annual World Hello Day. Anyone can
participate in World Hello Day simply by greeting ten people. This
demonstrates the importance of personal communication for preserving
peace. World Hello Day was begun in response to the conflict between Egypt
and Israel in the fall of 1973. Since then, World Hello Day has been observed
by people in 180 countries. People around the world use the occasion of
World Hello Day as an opportunity to express their concern for world peace.
Beginning with a simple greeting on World Hello Day, their activities send a
message to leaders, encouraging them to use communication rather than
force to settle conflicts. As a global event World Hello Day joins local
participation in a global expression of peace. 31 winners of the Nobel Peace
Prize are among the people who have realized World Hello Day's value as an
instrument for preserving peace and as an occasion that makes it possible for

anyone in the world to contribute to the process of creating peace. Brian McCormack, a Ph.D. graduate of Arizona State University, and Michael McCormack, a graduate of Harvard University, work together to promote this annual global event.

【101 年學測】閱讀測驗：31-40 出題來源

Digital Typhoon: Typhoon Names

Typhoons are named after number-based conventions and a list-based convention. The latter convention is more popular in most countries, such as human names for hurricanes, while the former is popular in Japan. Both conventions, however, share the same problem of ambiguity.

:

Number-based conventions are based on the sequential number from the beginning of a typhoon season. For example, Typhoon No. 14 is the 14th typhoon of the typhoon season. This kind of simplified 2-digit convention like "Typhoon No. 14" is very popular in Japan, often used in the media such as newspaper and television. This name does not the represent the year, because at the time of usage the current year is obvious.

:

List-based conventions are based on the list of typhoon names defined in advance by the committee of meteorological organizations worldwide. A new name is automatically chosen from the list upon the genesis of a typhoon. The list is defined for each basin and managed by the meteorological organization responsible for the respective basin. For example, Typhoon 200314 has a name "Maemi," which means a cicada or a locust in North Korea, and is an Asian name chosen from the list of typhoon names for the Western North Pacific basin.

:

【101 年學測】閱讀測驗：41-44 出題來源——Wikipedia

Kilt

The kilt is a knee-length garment with pleats at the rear, originating in the traditional dress of men and boys in the Scottish Highlands of the 16th century. Since the 19th century it has become associated with the wider culture of Scotland in general, or with Celtic (and more specifically Gaelic) heritage even more broadly. It is most often made of woollen cloth in a tartan pattern.

Although the kilt is most often worn on formal occasions and at Highland games and sports events, it has also been adapted as an item of fashionable informal male clothing in recent years, returning to its roots as an everyday garment.

⋮

【101 年學測】閱讀測驗：45-48 出題來源之一

Wesla Whitfield

Wesla Whitfield is a remarkable singer, with a deep love for that rich storehouse of musical treasures often identified as The Great American Popular Songbook.

Wesla has been developing her skills and learning her demanding craft for a number of years - by her own estimate, it's been ever since she "knew at age two-and-a-half that I would grow up to be a singer."

Her sound and approach would seem to place her somewhere in the intriguing area that borders on both jazz and that aspect of pop music which draws its material largely from the great standards and neglected gems of such as Cole Porter and Irving Berlin and Rodgers and Hart.

⋮

【101 年學測】閱讀測驗：49-52 出題來源

A History of Dining Utensils

⋮

Kitchen forks trace their origins back to the time of the Greeks. These forks were fairly large with two tines that aided in the carving and serving of meat. The tines prevented meat from twisting or moving during carving and allowed food to slide off more easily than it would with a knife.

By the 7th Century CE, royal courts of the Middle East began to use forks at the table for dining. From the 10th through the 13th Centuries, forks were fairly common among the wealthy in Byzantium.

⋮

In 1560, according to a French manners book, different customs evolved in different European countries. For eating soup, Germans are known for using spoons, Italians are known for using forks (presumably the fork assists in eating solid ingredients and the remaining liquid is drunk out of the bowl as it was in the Middle Ages). The Germans and Italians provide a knife for each diner, while the French provide only two or three communal knives for the whole table.

An Englishman named Thomas Coryate brought the first forks to England around 1611 after seeing them in Italy during his travels in 1608.

【101 年學測】閱讀測驗：53-56 出題來源

Photographing Animals

Animals are a favorite subject of many young photographers. Cats, dogs, hamsters and other pets top the list, followed by zoo animals and the occasional lizard.

Because it's hard to get them to sit still and "perform on command," many professional photographers joke that-given a choice-they will refuse to photograph pets or small children. There are ways around the problem of short attention spans, however.

One way to get an appealing portrait of a cat or dog is to hold a biscuit or treat above the camera. The animal's longing look toward the food will be captured by the camera as a soulful gaze. Because it's above the camera-out of the camera's range-the treat won't appear in the picture. When you show the picture to your friends afterwards, they will be impressed by your pet's loving expression.

If you are using fast film, you can take some good, quick shots of pets by simply snapping a picture right after calling their names. You'll get a different expression from your pets using this technique. Depending on your pet's disposition, the picture will capture an inquisitive expression or possibly a look of annoyance-especially if you've awakened Rover from a nap!

To photograph zoo animals, put the camera as close to the animal's cage as possible so you can shoot between the bars or wire mesh. Wild animals don't respond the same way as pets-after all, they don't know you! - so you will have to be more patient to capture a good shot. If it's legal to feed the animals, you can get their attention by having a friend toss them treats as you concentrate on shooting some good picture.

101年學測英文科非選擇題閱卷評分原則說明

閱卷召集人：賴惠玲（國立政治大學英文系教授）

　　101 學年度學科能力測驗英文考科的非選擇題題型共有兩大題，第一大題是中譯英，考生需將兩個中文句子譯成正確而通順達意的英文，題型與過去幾年相同，兩題合計八分。第二大題是英文作文，此次的題型為書信寫作，評量考生運用所學詞彙、句法寫出切合主題，並妥適達成特定溝通目的的書信；此次的主題是，考生最好的朋友沈迷於電玩，因此常常熬夜，疏忽課業並受到父母責罵，考生需寫一封文長至少120 個單詞（words）的信給他／她，給予適當勸告。作文滿分為二十分。

　　關於閱卷籌備工作，在正式閱卷前，於1 月 31 日先召開評分標準訂定會議，由正、副召集人及協同主持人共十四人，參閱了約 3000 份的試卷，經過一天的討論，訂定評分標準，選出合適的樣本，編製閱卷參考手冊，供閱卷委員共同參閱。

　　2 月 2 日上午 9：00 到11：00，168 位大學教授，分組進行試閱會議，根據閱卷參考手冊的樣卷，分別評分，並討論評分準則，務求評分標準一致，確保閱卷品質。為求慎重，試閱會議之後，正、副召集人及協同主持人進行評分標準再確定會議，確認評分原則後才開始正式閱卷。

　　關於評分標準，在中譯英部分，每小題總分 4 分，原則上是每個錯誤扣 0.5 分。作文的評分標準是依據內容、組織、文法句構、詞彙拼字、體例五個項目給分，字數明顯不足則扣總分1 分。

閱卷時，每份試卷皆會經過兩位委員分別評分，最後以二人平均分數計算。如果第一閱與第二閱分數差距超過標準，將再由第三位委員（正、副召集人或協同主持人）評閱。

今年的中譯英與國片有關，句型及詞彙皆爲高中生所熟悉；評量的重點在於考生能否能運用熟悉的詞彙與基本句型將中文翻譯成正確達意的英文句子，所測驗之詞彙皆控制在大考中心詞彙表四級內之詞彙，中等程度以上的考生如果能使用正確句型並注意用字、拼字，應能得理想的分數；但在選取樣卷時發現，很多考生對於英文詞彙的使用及中英文句構之間的差異，仍有加強的空間，如中文裡「臺灣製作的影片」譯成英文時爲 movies/films produced in Taiwan，兩者詞序不同；「受到國際的重視」的翻譯應爲 have attracted international attention;「拍攝這些電影的地點」譯成英文時的關係子句及被動語態結構 the locations where these films were shot 與中文有差異，考生仍須加強這些用字及句構的掌握。

英文作文題目的主題與考生的生活經驗息息相關，考生大多能發揮，由於是書信寫作，如果書信格式使用不當或未按照規定使用所提供之英文名字，會酌予扣分；書信內容是爲了勸告最好的朋友不要再沈迷於電玩，大部分考生均能就個人經驗表達，評分的考量主要爲內容是否能鋪陳書信的溝通目的並對朋友提出具體勸告，組織連慣性、句子結構及用字適切與否、以及拼字與標點符號的正確使用等。

101年學測英文科試題或答案之反映意見回覆

※ 題號：30

【題目】

In the fall of 1973, in an effort to bring attention to the conflict between Egypt and Israel, *World Hello Day* was born. The objective is to promote peace all over the world, and to ___26___ barriers between every nationality. Since then, *World Hello Day*——November 21st of every year—— ___27___ observed by people in 180 countries.

Taking part couldn't be ___28___. All one has to do is say hello to 10 people on the day. However, in response to the ___29___ of this event, the concepts of fostering peace and harmony do not have to be confined to one day a year. We can ___30___ the spirit going by communicating often and consciously. It is a simple act that anyone can do and it reminds us that communication is more effective than conflict.

30. (A) push   (B) keep
    (C) bring   (D) make

【意見內容】

選項 (C) 應為合理答案。文章可解釋為 We can bring the spirit (which is going) by communication often and consciously，亦符合文意。

【大考中心意見回覆】

本題評量考生能否掌握 keep *sth.* going 的用法。本題作答線索在於全文文意的理解以及空格後 ...the spirit going。選項 (C) bring 無論在用法或者是語意上皆與本文無關，故非本題正答。

※ 題號：34

【題目】

　　Generally there are two ways to name typhoons: the number-based convention and the list-based convention. Following the number-based convention, typhoons are coded with ___31___ types of numbers such as a 4-digit or a 6-digit code. For example, the 14th typhoon in 2003 can be labeled either as Typhoon 0314 or Typhoon 200314. The ___32___ of this convention, however, is that a number is hard to remember. The list-based convention, on the other hand, is based on the list of typhoon names compiled in advance by a committee, and is more widely used.

　　At the very beginning, only ___33___ names were used because at that time typhoons were named after girlfriends or wives of the experts on the committee. In 1979, however, male names were also included because women protested against the original naming ___34___ for reasons of gender equality.

　　In Asia, Western names were used until 2000 when the committee decided to use Asian names to ___35___ Asians' awareness of typhoons. The names were chosen from a name pool ___36___ of 140 names, 10 each from the 14 members of the committee. Each country has its unique naming preferences. Korea and Japan ___37___ animal names and China likes names of gods such as Longwang (dragon king) and Fengshen (god of the wind).

After the 140 names are all used in order, they will be ___38___. But the names can be changed. If a member country suffers great damage from a certain typhoon, it can ___39___ that the name of the typhoon be deleted from the list at the annual committee meeting. For example, the names of Nabi by South Korea, and Longwang by China were ___40___ with other names in 2007. The deletion of both names was due to the severe damage caused by the typhoons bearing the names.

(A) request　　(B) favor　　(C) disadvantage　　(D) composed
(E) recycled　　(F) practice　　(G) replaced　　(H) raise
(I) various　　(J) female

【意見內容】

選項 (B) 應為合理答案。選項 (B) favor 與選項 (D) practice 均各自有動詞、名詞形式，若第 34 題先填入 (B) favor，表示「（命名的）偏好」，而第 37 題則填入 (F) practice 則表示「實行、實施」，更有解釋空間。

【大考中心意見回覆】

本題在於評量考生依據上下文意，掌握名詞 practice 的語意及用法。作答線索在於空格前文意的掌握，尤其是在第二段第一句 At the very beginning...were named after girlfriends or wives...。考生若能掌握 At the very beginning 呼應 original，而 named after girlfriends or wives 呼應 naming practice，便能正確作答。favor 無法與 naming 連用，亦無法與空格後 for reasons of gender equality 之文意相連貫，故本題最適當答案為選項 (F) practice。

※ 題號：42

【題目】

41-44 為題組

　　The kilt is a skirt traditionally worn by Scottish men. It is a tailored garment that is wrapped around the wearer's body at the waist starting from one side, around the front and back and across the front again to the opposite side. The overlapping layers in front are called "aprons." Usually, the kilt covers the body from the waist down to just above the knees. A properly made kilt should not be so loose that the wearer can easily twist the kilt around the body, nor should it be so tight that it causes bulging of the fabric where it is buckled. Underwear may be worn as one prefers.

　　One of the most distinctive features of the kilt is the pattern of squares, or sett, it exhibits. The association of particular patterns with individual families can be traced back hundreds of years. Then in the Victorian era (19th century), weaving companies began to systematically record and formalize the system of setts for commercial purposes. Today there are also setts for States and Provinces, schools and universities, and general patterns that anybody can wear.

　　The kilt can be worn with accessories. On the front apron, there is often a kilt pin, topped with a small decorative family symbol. A small knife can be worn with the kilt too. It typically comes in a very wide variety, from fairly plain to quite elaborate silver- and jewel-ornamented designs. The kilt can also be worn with a sporran, which is the Gaelic word for pouch or purse.

42. Which of the following is a correct description about setts?

(A) They were once symbols for different Scottish families.

(B) They were established by the government for business purposes.

(C) They represented different States and Provinces in the 19th century.

(D) They used to come in one general pattern for all individuals and institutions.

【意見內容】

根據文章中 Today there are also setts for States and Provinces, schools and universities, and general patterns that anybody can wear. 呼應選項 (D) They used to come in one general pattern for all individuals and institutions. ，因此判斷選項 (D) 應為合理答案。

【大考中心意見回覆】

本題測驗考生掌握文章的內容細節的能力。作答線索在第二段，尤其是第二句 The association of particular patterns with individual families can be traced back hundreds of years. 。根據文章第二段內容，選項 (D) 中 …one general pattern for all individuals and institutions 的敘述與本段文意不符，從最後一句 Today there are also setts for States and Provinces, schools and universities, and general patterns that anybody can wear. 即可判斷選項 (D) 非正確之選項，故選項 (A) 為本題正答無誤。

※ 題號：43

【題目】

41-44 為題組

The kilt is a skirt traditionally worn by Scottish men. It is a tailored garment that is wrapped around the wearer's body at the waist starting from one side, around the front and back and across the front again to the opposite side. The overlapping layers in front are called "aprons." Usually, the kilt covers the body from the waist down to just above the knees. A properly made kilt should not be so loose that the wearer can easily twist the kilt around the body, nor should it be so tight that it causes bulging of the fabric where it is buckled. Underwear may be worn as one prefers.

One of the most distinctive features of the kilt is the pattern of squares, or sett, it exhibits. The association of particular patterns with individual families can be traced back hundreds of years. Then in the Victorian era (19th century), weaving companies began to systematically record and formalize the system of setts for commercial purposes. Today there are also setts for States and Provinces, schools and universities, and general patterns that anybody can wear.

The kilt can be worn with accessories. On the front apron, there is often a kilt pin, topped with a small decorative family symbol. A small knife can be worn with the kilt too. It typically comes in a very wide variety, from fairly plain to quite elaborate silver- and jewel-ornamented designs. The kilt can also be worn with a sporran, which is the Gaelic word for pouch or purse.

43. Which of the following items is **NOT** typically worn with the kilt for decoration?
    (A) A pin.　　　　　　　　(B) A purse.
    (C) A ruby apron.　　　　　(D) A silver knife..

【意見內容】

根據文章最後一段的敘述，pin 是配件，上面可以放置族徽等飾品，
但沒指名 pin 就是飾品，因此選項 (A) 應為本題答案。

【大考中心意見回覆】

本題測驗考生能否掌握文章內容細節之間的關係。作答線索在第三
段內容。第三段主題句 The kilt can be worn with accessories 已經點
出本段相關細節內容。本題所問的是下列選項中何者不是蘇格蘭裙
上的裝飾品，由第二個句子中的 …there is often a kilt pin, topped
with a small decorative family symbol 已可判斷選項 (A) A pin 為正確
訊息，而第三句 a small knife 與第五句的 pouch or purse 顯示選項
(B) 與選項 (D) 為正確訊息，但全文內容並未提及 ruby apron 相關之
訊息，故選項 (C) 為本題正答。

※ 題號：46

【題目】

45-48 為題組

Wesla Whitfield, a famous jazz singer, has a unique style and life
story, so I decided to see one of her performances and interview
her for my column.

　　I went to a nightclub in New York and watched the stage
lights go up. After the band played an introduction, Wesla
Whitfield wheeled herself onstage in a wheelchair. As she sang,
Whitfield's voice was so powerful and soulful that everyone in
the room forgot the wheelchair was even there.

　　At 57, Whitfield is small and pretty, witty and humble,
persistent and philosophical. Raised in California, Whitfield
began performing in public at age 18, when she took a job as a
singing waitress at a pizza parlor. After studying classical music

in college, she moved to San Francisco and went on to sing with the San Francisco Opera Chorus.

Walking home from rehearsal at age 29, she was caught in the midst of a random shooting that left her paralyzed from the waist down. I asked how she dealt with the realization that she'd never walk again, and she confessed that initially she didn't want to face it. After a year of depression she tried to kill herself. She was then admitted to a hospital for treatment, where she was able to recover.

Whitfield said she came to understand that the only thing she had lost in this misfortunate event was the ability to walk. She still possessed her most valuable asset——her mind. Pointing to her head, she said, "Everything important is in here. The only real disability in life is losing your mind." When I asked if she was angry about what she had lost, she admitted to being frustrated occasionally, "especially when everybody's dancing, because I love to dance. But **when that happens** I just remove myself so I can focus instead on what I can do."

46. What does "**when that happens**" mean in the last paragraph?
    (A) When Wesla is losing her mind.
    (B) When Wesla is singing on the stage.
    (C) When Wesla is going out in her wheelchair.
    (D) When Wesla is watching other people dancing.

【意見內容】

根據前兩段內容指出，Whitfield 有時會因爲失去控制雙腿的能力而感到生氣沮喪，「特別是」當大家都在跳舞時，由此並不能解讀只有在大家都跳舞才有這種想法，應該是前面文章所提的她仍有最有價值的 mind，選項 (A) 應爲最佳答案。

【大考中心意見回覆】

本題測驗考生根據上下文意掌握文中指代詞（anaphora）的能力。
作答線索在最後一段倒數第二句 When I asked if she was angry about
what she had lost, ...especially when everybody's dancing, because I
love to dance. But...；本段前文的文意亦為作答線索。選項 (A) When
Welsa is losing her mind. 與本段文意不符，故選項 (D) When Welsa is
watching other people dancing. 為本題正答無誤。

※ 題號：49

【題目】

49-52 為題組

Forks trace their origins back to the ancient Greeks. Forks at
that time were fairly large with two tines that aided in the carving
of meat in the kitchen. The tines prevented meat from twisting or
moving during carving and allowed food to slide off more easily
than it would with a knife.

By the 7th century A.D., royal courts of the Middle East began
to use forks at the table for dining. From the 10th through the 13th
centuries, forks were fairly common among the wealthy in
Byzantium. In the 11th century, a Byzantine wife brought forks to
Italy; however, they were not widely adopted there until the 16th
century. Then in 1533, forks were brought from Italy to France.
The French were also slow to accept forks, for using them was
thought to be awkward.

In 1608, forks were brought to England by Thomas Coryate,
who saw them during his travels in Italy. The English first

ridiculed forks as being unnecessary. "Why should a person need a fork when God had given him hands?" they asked. Slowly, however, forks came to be adopted by the wealthy as a symbol of their social status. They were prized possessions made of expensive materials intended to impress guests. By the mid 1600s, eating with forks was considered fashionable among the wealthy British.

Early table forks were modeled after kitchen forks, but small pieces of food often fell through the two tines or slipped off easily. In late 17th century France, larger forks with four curved tines were developed. The additional tines made diners less likely to drop food, and the curved tines served as a scoop so people did not have to constantly switch to a spoon while eating. By the early 19th century, four-tined forks had also been developed in Germany and England and slowly began to spread to America.

49. What is the passage mainly about?
    (A) The different designs of forks.
    (B) The spread of fork-aided cooking.
    (C) The history of using forks for dining.
    (D) The development of fork-related table manners.

【意見內容】

根據文章第一段第一句 Forks at that time were fairly large with two tines that aided in the carving of meat in the kitchen. ，以及最後一段 ...larger forks with four curved tines were developed 可知叉子設計的改變，因此選項 (A) 應為合理答案。

【大考中心意見回覆】

本題測驗考生掌握文章主旨的能力。作答線索遍及全文，尤其各段的主題句提供了本題作答的關鍵。選項 (A) The different designs of forks 僅是本文內容的一部分並非全文主旨，因此選項 (C) The history of using forks for dining. 為本題正答無誤。

※ 題號：54

【題目】

53-56 為題組

Animals are a favorite subject of many photographers. Cats, dogs, and other pets top the list, followed by zoo animals. However, because it's hard to get them to sit still and "perform on command," some professional photographers refuse to photograph pets.

One way to get an appealing portrait of a cat or dog is to hold a biscuit or treat above the camera. The animal's longing look toward the food will be captured by the camera, but the treat won't appear in the picture because it's out of the camera's range. When you show the picture to your friends afterwards, they'll be impressed by your pet's loving expression.

If you are using fast film, you can take some good, quick shots of a pet by simply snapping a picture right after calling its name. You'll get a different expression from your pet using this technique. Depending on your pet's mood, the picture will capture an interested, curious expression or possibly a look of annoyance, especially if you've awakened it from a nap.

Taking pictures of zoo animals requires a little more patience. After all, you can't wake up a lion! You may have to wait for a while until the animal does something interesting or moves into a position for you to get a good shot. When photographing zoo animals, don't get too close to the cages, and never tap on the glass or throw things between the bars of a cage. Concentrate on shooting some good pictures, and always respect the animals you are photographing.

54. What is the use of a biscuit in taking pictures of a pet?
    (A) To capture a cute look.
    (B) To create a special atmosphere.
    (C) To arouse the appetite of the pet.
    (D) To keep the pet from looking at the camera.

【意見內容】

1. 選項 (C) 應為合理答案。

    (1) 選項 (A) To capture a cute look 為間接用途，選項 (C) 為直接用途。

    (2) 由該段最後一句中的 loving expression 回指第二句 …animal's longing look forward the food，因拍攝過程中餅乾的主要功能應為「引起寵物的食慾以吸引其注意」。

    (3) 小餅乾的直接用途應該是勾起寵物的食慾，間接讓牠們靜止不動，而不是拿來拍照。

    (4) Appetite 除了做「胃口」解釋外，也可代表「興致、愛好」的意思。文章中的 longing expression toward the food 應是對食物有了興致。

2. 選項 (A) 語意不清。

【大考中心意見回覆】

1. 本題測驗考生掌握文章內容細節之間關係的能力。作答線索在第二段第一句及最後一句 loving expression。本題題幹中已明白說明 the use of a biscuit in taking pictures，且根據第二段第一句 One way to get an appealing portrait of a cat or dog is to hold a biscuit or treat above the camera. 可知，拿著餅乾的目的不是引起寵物的食慾，而是拍得一張動人的照片（to get an appealing portrait）、捕捉可愛的表情（loving expression/a cute look）。再者，appetite 若要當「興致、愛好」解釋，應該與介系詞for 搭配使用，而非介系詞of 連用，因此本題選項 (C) 中的appetite 一詞應單指「食慾」之意。

2. 「to」即有表達「目的」的意思，因此無論有沒有加 help 一詞，選項 (A) To capture a cute look 的語意皆明確、無誤。

※ 題號：非選擇題一、第 1 小題、第 2 小題

【題目】

1. 近年來，許多臺灣製作的影片已經受到國際的重視。
2. 拍攝這些電影的地點也成為熱門的觀光景點。

提示： 請仔細觀察以下三幅連環圖片的內容，並想像第四幅圖片可能的發展，寫出一個涵蓋連環圖片內容並有完整結局的故事。

【意見內容】

中譯英第 1、2 題參考答案之正確性。

【大考中心意見回覆】

非選擇題的評分標準說明將刊登於本中心網頁，敬請參考，謝謝。

101 年大學入學學科能力測驗試題
數學考科

第壹部分：選擇題（佔 65 分）

一、單選題（佔 35 分）

說明：第 1 題至第 7 題，每題有 5 個選項，其中只有一個是正確或最適當的
選項，請畫記在答案卡之「選擇（填）題答案區」。各題答對者，
得 5 分；答錯、未作答或畫記多於一個選項者，該題以零分計算。

1. $\sqrt{\dfrac{1}{5^2}+\dfrac{1}{4^2}+1}$ 等於下列哪一個選項？

　(1) 1.01　　　(2) 1.05　　　(3) 1.1　　　(4) 1.15　　　(5) 1.21

2. 將邊長為 1 公分的正力方體堆疊成一階梯形立體，如下圖所示，
其中第 1 層（最下層）有 10 塊，第 2 層有 9 塊，…，依此類推。
當堆疊完 10 層時，該階梯形立體的表面積（即該立體的前、後、
上、下、左、右各表面的面積總和）為多少？

　(1) 75 平方公分　　　　　(2) 90 平方公分
　(3) 110 平方公分　　　　 (4) 130 平方公分
　(5) 150 平方公分

3. 下表為常用對數表 $\log_{10} N$ 的一部分：

N	0	1	2	3	4	5	6	7	8	9
10	0000	0043	0086	0128	1070	0212	0253	0294	2334	0374
11	0414	0453	0492	0531	0569	0607	0645	0682	0719	0755
⋮	⋮	⋮	⋮	⋮	⋮	⋮	⋮	⋮	⋮	⋮
20	3010	3032	3054	3075	3096	3118	3139	3160	3181	3201
⋮	⋮	⋮	⋮	⋮	⋮	⋮	⋮	⋮	⋮	⋮
30	4771	4786	4800	4814	4829	4843	4857	4871	4886	4900

請問 $10^{3.032}$ 最接近下列哪一個選項？

(1) 101　　(2) 201　　(3) 1007　　(4) 1076　　(5) 2012

4. 甲、乙兩校有一樣多的學生參加數學能力測驗，兩校學生測驗成績的分布都很接近常態分布，其中甲校學生的平均分數為 60 分，標準差為 10 分；乙校學生的平均分數為 65 分，標準差為 5 分。若用粗線表示甲校學生成績分布曲線；細線表示乙校學生成績分布曲線，則下列哪一個分布圖較為正確？

(1)

(2)

(3)

(4)

(5)

5. 若正實數 x, y 滿足 $\log_{10} x = 2.8$，$\log_{10} y = 5.6$，則 $\log10\,(x^2 + y)$ 最接近下列哪一個選項的值？

(1) 2.8　　(2) 5.6　　(3) 5.9　　(4) 8.4　　(5) 11.2

6. 箱中有編號分別為 0, 1, 2, ..., 9 的十顆球。隨機抽取一球，將球放回後，再隨機抽取一球。請問這兩球編號相減的絕對值為下列哪一個選項時，其出現的機率最大？

(1) 0　　(2) 1　　(3) 4　　(4) 5　　(5) 9

7. 空間坐標中有一球面（半徑大於 0）與平面 $3x + 4y = 0$ 相切於原點，請問此球面與三個坐標軸一共有多少個交點？

(1) 1　　(2) 2　　(3) 3　　(4) 4　　(5) 5

二、**多選題**（佔 30 分）

說明：第 8 題至第 13 題，每題有 5 個選項，其中至少有一個是正確的選項，請將正確選項畫記在答案卡之「選擇（填）題答案區」。各題之選項獨立判定，所有選項均答對者，得 5 分；答錯 1 個選項者，得 3 分；答錯 2 個選項者，得 1 分；答錯多於 2 個選項或所有選項均未作答者，該題以零分計算。

8. 設 $f(x) = x^4 - 5x^3 + x^2 + ax + b$ 為實係數多項式，且知 $f(i) = 0$（其中 $i^2 = -1$）。請問下列哪些選項是多項式方程式 $f(x) = 0$ 的根？

   (1) $-i$　　　(2) 0　　　(3) 1　　　(4) -5　　　(5) 5

9. 三角形 ABC 是一個邊長為 3 的正三角形，如下圖所示。若在每一邊的兩個三等分點中，各選取一點連成三角形，則下列哪些選項是正確的？

   (1) 以此方法可能連成的三角形一共有 8 個

   (2) 這些可能連成的三角形中，恰有 2 個是銳角三角形

   (3) 這些可能連成的三角形中，恰有 3 個是直角三角形

   (4) 這些可能連成的三角形中，恰有 3 個是鈍角三角形

   (5) 這些可能連成的三角形中，恰有 1 個是正三角形

10. 設 O 為複數平面上的原點，並令點 A, B 分別代表非零複數 z, w。若 $\angle AOB = 90°$，則下列哪些選項必為**負實數**？

   (1) $\dfrac{z}{w}$　　　　　　　　(2) zw

   (3) $(zw)^2$　　　　　　　(4) $\dfrac{z^2}{w^2}$

   (5) $\left(z\overline{w}\right)^2$　（其中 $\overline{w}$ 為 w 的共軛複數）

11. 若實數 a, b, c, d 使得聯立方程組 $\begin{cases} ax + 8y = c \\ x - 4y = 3 \end{cases}$ 有解，且聯立方程

組 $\begin{cases} -3x + by = d \\ x - 4y = 3 \end{cases}$ 無解，則下列哪些選項一定正確？

(1) $a \neq -2$ (2) $c = -6$

(3) $b = 12$ (4) $d \neq -9$

(5) 聯立方程組 $\begin{cases} ax + 8y = c \\ -3x + by = d \end{cases}$ 無解

12. 在坐標平面上，廣義角 θ 的頂點為原點 O，始邊為 x 軸的正向，

且滿足 $\tan \theta = \dfrac{2}{3}$。若 θ 的終邊上有一點 P，其 y 坐標為 -4，則下

列哪些選項一定正確？

(1) P 的 x 坐標是 6   (2) $\overline{OP} = 2\sqrt{13}$

(3) $\cos \theta = \dfrac{3}{\sqrt{13}}$ (4) $\sin 2\theta > 0$

(5) $\cos \dfrac{\theta}{2} < 0$

13. 平面上兩點 F_1, F_2 滿足 $\overline{F_1 F_2} = 4$。設 d 為一實數，令 Γ 表示平面上

滿足 $\left| \overline{PF_1} - \overline{PF_2} \right| = d$ 的所有 P 點所成的圖形，又令 C 為平面上以 F_1

為圓心，6 為半徑的圓。請問下列哪些選項是正確的？

(1) 當 $d = 0$ 時，Γ 為直線

(2) 當 $d = 1$ 時，Γ 為雙曲線

(3) 當 $d = 2$ 時，Γ 與圓 C 交於兩點

(4) 當 $d = 4$ 時，Γ 與圓 C 交於四點

(5) 當 $d = 8$ 時，Γ 不存在

第貳部分：選填題（佔 35 分）

說明：1. 第 A 至 G 題，將答案畫記在答案卡之「選擇（填）題答案
　　　　區」所標示的列號（14–33）。

　　　2. 每題完全答對給 5 分，答錯不倒扣，未完全答對不給分。

A. 若首項爲 a、公比爲 0.01 的無窮等比級數和等於循環小數 $1.\overline{2}$，
　則 $a =$ ⑭.⑮⑯ 。

B. 設 $A(1,1)$，$B(3,5)$，$C(5,3)$，$D(0,-7)$，$E(2,-3)$ 及 $F(8,-6)$ 爲坐標平
　面上的六個點。若直線 L 分別與三角形 ABC 及三角形 DEF 各恰
　有一個交點，則 L 的斜率之最小可能值爲 ⑰⑱ 。

C. 小明在天文網站上看到以下的資訊「可利用北斗七星斗杓的天璇
　與天樞這兩顆星來尋找北極星：由天璇起始向天樞的方向延伸便
　可找到北極星，其中天樞與北極星的距離爲天樞與天璇距離的 5
　倍。」今小明將所見的星空想像成一個坐標平面，其中天璇的坐
　標爲 (9,8) 及天樞的坐標爲 (7,11)。依上述資訊可以推得北極星的
　坐標爲（ ⑲⑳ , ㉑㉒ 。）

D. 設點 $A(-2,2)$、$B(4,8)$ 爲坐標平面上兩點，且點 C 在二次函數
　$y = \dfrac{1}{2}x^2$ 的圖形上變動。當 C 點的 x 坐標爲 ㉓㉔ 時，內積
　$\overrightarrow{AB} \cdot \overrightarrow{AC}$ 有最小值 ㉕㉖ 。

E. 在邊長為 13 的正三角形 *ABC* 上各邊分別取一點 *P* , *Q* , *R*，使得 *APQR* 形成一平行四邊形，如下圖所示：

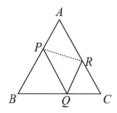

若平行四邊形 *APQR* 的面積為 $20\sqrt{3}$，則線段 *PR* 的長度為 ㉗ 。

F. 設 *m* , *n* 為正實數，橢圓 $\dfrac{x^2}{m} + \dfrac{y^2}{n} = 1$ 的焦點分別為 $F_1(0,2)$ 與 $F_2(0,-2)$。若此橢圓尚有一點 *P* 使得 ΔPF_1F_2 為一正三角形，則 *m* = ㉘㉙ ， *n* = ㉚㉛ 。

G. 坐標空間中，在六個平面 $x = \dfrac{14}{13}$, $x = \dfrac{1}{13}$, $y = 1$, $y = -1$, $z = -1$ 及 $z = -4$ 所圍成的長方體上隨機選取兩個相異頂點。若每個頂點被選取的機率相同，則選到兩個頂點的距離大於 3 之機率為 $\dfrac{㉜}{㉝}$ 。（化成最簡分數）

參考公式及可能用到的數值

1. 一元二次方程式 $ax^2 + bx + c = 0$ 的公式解：

$$x = \frac{-b \pm \sqrt{b^2 - 4ac}}{2a}$$

2. 平面上兩點 $P_1(x_1, y_1)$，$P_2(x_2, y_2)$ 間的距離為

$$\overline{P_1P_2} = \sqrt{(x_2 - x_1)^2 + (y_2 - y_1)^2}$$

3. 通過 (x_1, y_1) 與 (x_2, y_2) 的直線斜率 $m = \dfrac{y_2 - y_1}{x_2 - x_1}$，$x_2 \neq x_1$

4. 首項為 a_1，公差為 d 的等差數列前 n 項之和為

$$S = \frac{n(a_1 - a_n)}{2} = \frac{n(2a_1 + (n-1)d)}{2}$$

等比數列 $\langle ar^{k-1} \rangle$ 的前 n 項之和　$S_n = \dfrac{a(1 - r^n)}{1 - r}$，$r \neq 1$

5. 級數公式：$\displaystyle\sum_{k=1}^{n} k^2 = 1^2 + 2^2 + 3^2 + \cdots + n^2 = \frac{n(n+1)(2n+1)}{6}$

6. 三角函數的和角公式：　$\sin(A + B) = \sin A \cos B + \sin B \cos A$

$$\cos(A + B) = \cos A \cos B - \sin A \sin B$$

7. $\triangle ABC$ 的正弦定理： $\dfrac{a}{\sin A} = \dfrac{b}{\sin B} = \dfrac{c}{\sin C} = 2R$ ，

R 為 $\triangle ABC$ 的外接圓半徑

$\triangle ABC$ 的餘弦定理： $c^2 = a^2 + b^2 - 2ab\cos C$

8. 棣美弗定理：設 $z = r(\cos\theta + i\sin\theta)$ ，則 $z^n = r^n(\cos n\theta + i\sin n\theta)$ ，n 為一正整數

9. 算術平均數： $M(= \overline{X}) = \dfrac{1}{n}(x_1 + x_2 + \cdots + x_n) = \dfrac{1}{n}\sum_{i=1}^{n} x_i$

（樣本）標準差： $S = \sqrt{\dfrac{1}{n-1}\sum_{i=1}^{n}(x_i - \overline{X})^2} = \sqrt{\dfrac{1}{n-1}\left(\left(\sum_{i=1}^{n} x_i^2\right) - n\overline{X}^2\right)}$

10. 95% 信心水準下的信賴區間： $\left[\hat{p} - 2\sqrt{\dfrac{\hat{p}(1-\hat{p})}{n}},\ \hat{p} + 2\sqrt{\dfrac{\hat{p}(1-\hat{p})}{n}}\right]$

11. 參考數值： $\sqrt{2} \approx 1.414$ ， $\sqrt{3} \approx 1.732$ ， $\sqrt{5} \approx 2.236$ ， $\sqrt{6} \approx 2.449$ ，$\pi \approx 3.142$

12. 對數值： $\log_{10} 2 \approx 0.3010$ ， $\log_{10} 3 \approx 0.4771$ ， $\log_{10} 5 \approx 0.6990$ ，$\log_{10} 7 \approx 0.8451$

101年度學科能力測驗數學科試題詳解

第壹部分：選擇題

一、單選擇

1. 【答案】(2)

　　【解析】 $\sqrt{\dfrac{4^2+5^2+5^2\cdot 4^2}{5^2\cdot 4^2}}=\sqrt{\dfrac{441}{400}}=\dfrac{21}{20}=1.05$，故選 (2)。

2. 【答案】(5)

　　【解析】 上＋下＋左＋右：4×10

　　　　　　前＋後：$2(1+2\cdots+10)=2\cdot\dfrac{10\cdot(1+10)}{2}=110$

　　　　　　$40+110=150$　　　　故選 (5)

3. 【答案】(4)

　　【解析】 $a=b\times 10^n=10^{3.032}$　$\Rightarrow$　$\log a=n+\log b=3+0.032$

　　　　　(1) a 為 $3+1$ 位數

　　　　　(2) $\begin{cases} \log 1.07=0.0294 \\ \log b=0.0320 \\ \log 1.08=0.0334 \end{cases}$　$\Rightarrow$　$1.07<b<1.08$

　　　　　　$1070<a<1080$

4. 【答案】(1)

　　【解析】 甲較分散，算數平均數較小，乙較集中，算術平均數較
　　　　　　大，故選 (1)。

5. 【答案】(3)

 【解析】 $x = 10^{2.8}$，$y = 10^{5.6}$

 $log\,(x^2 + y) = log\,(10^{5.6} + 10^{5.6}) = log\,2 \cdot 10^{5.6}$

 $= (log\,2) + 5.6 \fallingdotseq 5.9$

6. 【答案】(2)

 【解析】 差 0：$\dfrac{10}{10 \cdot 10}$；差 1：$\dfrac{9 \cdot 2}{10 \cdot 10}$；差 2：$\dfrac{8 \cdot 2}{10 \cdot 10}$

 差 3：$\dfrac{7 \cdot 2}{10 \cdot 10}$；差 4：$\dfrac{6 \cdot 2}{10 \cdot 10}$；差 5：$\dfrac{5 \cdot 2}{10 \cdot 10}$

 差 6：$\dfrac{4 \cdot 2}{10 \cdot 10}$；差 7：$\dfrac{3 \cdot 2}{10 \cdot 10}$；差 8：$\dfrac{2 \cdot 2}{10 \cdot 10}$

 差 9：$\dfrac{1 \cdot 2}{10 \cdot 10}$，故差 1 最大。

7. 【答案】(3)

 【解析】 $\vec{n} = (3，4，0)$

 故此球與 x 軸 y 軸交 2 點，z 軸 1 點　　∴ 3 點

二、多選題

8. 【答案】(1)(2)(5)

 【解析】 $f(i) = i^4 - 5(i)^3 + i^2 + ai + b = b + (a+5)i = 0 + 0i$

 $\Rightarrow b = 0$，$a = -5$

 $f(x) = x^4 - 5x^3 + x^2 - 5x = x(x-5)(x^2+1)$

 故選 (1)(2)(5)

9. 【答案】(1) (2)

　　【解析】(1)　$2^3 = 8$

　　　　　　(2)　$y = \sqrt{2^2 + 1^2 - 2 \cdot 2 \cdot 1 \cdot \cos 60^\circ} = \sqrt{3}$

　　　　　　(3)

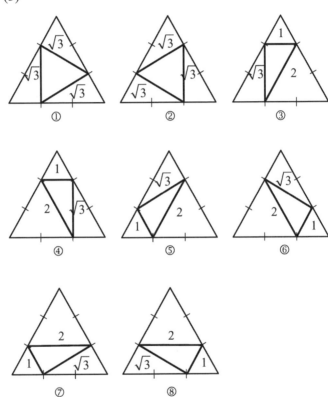

　　　　銳角三角形：2，直角三角形：6，

　　　　鈍角三角形：0，正三角形：2，

　　　　故選 (1) (2)。

10. 【答案】 (4) (5)

　　【解析】 $\dfrac{z}{w}=r\,(cos\,90^\circ+i\,sin\,90^\circ\,)=r\,i$

　　(1) $\dfrac{z}{w}=r\,i$，不眞

　　(2) $z\cdot w$ 無法確定，不眞

　　(3) $(z\cdot w)^2$ 無法確定，不眞

　　(4) $(\dfrac{z}{w})^2=r^2\cdot i^2=-r^2$，眞

　　(5) $w\cdot\overline{w}=|\,w\,|^2\ \Rightarrow\ \overline{w}=\dfrac{1}{w}\cdot\big|\,\overline{w}\,\big|^2$

　　　　$\Rightarrow\ (z\cdot\overline{w})^2=(\dfrac{z}{w})^2\,\big|\,\overline{w}\,\big|^2=-r^2\,\big|\,\overline{w}\,\big|^2$，眞。

11. 【答案】 (3) (4)

　　【解析】 $\begin{cases} a\,x+8\,y=c \\ x-4\,y=3 \end{cases}$ 有解 $\Rightarrow$ 恰1解或無限多組解

　　恰1解：$\triangle_1\ne0=\begin{vmatrix} a & 8 \\ 1 & -4 \end{vmatrix}\ \Rightarrow a\ne-2$

　　無限多組解：$\triangle_1=\triangle_{1x}=0\ \Rightarrow a=-2$，且 $c=-6$

　　$\begin{cases} -3\,x+b\,y=d \\ x-4\,y=3 \end{cases}$ 無解

　　$\Rightarrow\triangle_2=0=\begin{vmatrix} -3 & b \\ 1 & -4 \end{vmatrix}$ 且 $\triangle_{2y}\ne0=\begin{vmatrix} -3 & d \\ 1 & 3 \end{vmatrix}\Rightarrow b=12$

　　且 $d\ne-9$ 故 (3) (4) 正確。

　　$\begin{cases} a\,x+8\,y=c \\ x-4\,y=3 \end{cases}$ 有解，且 $\begin{cases} a\,x+8\,y=c \\ -3\,x+b\,y=a \end{cases}$ 無解

　　有兩種可能：

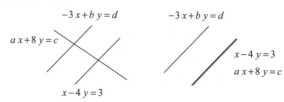

　　故 (5) 不正確。

12. 【答案】(2) (4)

　　【解析】$tan\theta = \dfrac{2}{3} = \dfrac{-4}{x} \Rightarrow x = -6 \Rightarrow P(-6，-4)$

　　　　(1)　$\times$

　　　　(2)　$\overline{OP} = \sqrt{6^2 + 4^2} = 2\sqrt{13}$

　　　　(3)　$cos\theta = \dfrac{-6}{2\sqrt{13}} = \dfrac{-3}{\sqrt{13}}$

　　　　(4)　$sin\theta = \dfrac{-2}{\sqrt{13}}$

　　　　　　$\Rightarrow sin2\theta = 2\,sin\theta\,cos\theta = 2 \cdot \dfrac{-2}{\sqrt{13}} \cdot \dfrac{-3}{\sqrt{13}} = \dfrac{12}{13} > 0$

　　　　(5)　$tan\theta > 0$，$sin\theta < 0 \Rightarrow \theta \in$ 第三象限

　　　　　　$180° + 360° \cdot k < \theta < 270° + 360° \cdot k \quad (k \in z)$

　　　　　　$\Rightarrow 90° + 180° \cdot k < \dfrac{\theta}{2} < 180° + 180° \cdot k$

　　　　　　$k = 0 \Rightarrow 90° < \dfrac{\theta}{2} < 135° \quad k = 1 \Rightarrow 270° < \dfrac{\theta}{2} < 315°$，

　　　　　　故不真。

13. 【答案】(1) (2) (5)

　　【解析】$d < 4 \Rightarrow P$ 為雙曲線與 C_1 有 4 個交點

　　　　　　$d = 4 \Rightarrow P$ 為 2 射線與 C_1 有 2 個交點

　　　　　　$d > 4 \Rightarrow P$ 無圖形

　　　　　　$d = 0 \Rightarrow P$ 為 $\overline{F_1F_2}$ 之中垂線與 C_1 有 2 交點

　　　　　　故選 (1) (2) (5)。

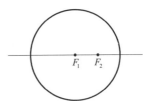

第貳部份：選填題

A. 【答案】 1.21

【解析】 $\dfrac{a}{1-0.01}=1.\overline{2}=1+\dfrac{2}{9}=\dfrac{11}{9}=\dfrac{a}{0.99}$

$\Rightarrow a=1.21$

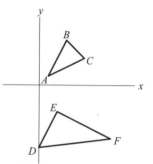

B. 【答案】 -3

【解析】 斜率最小為 $m_{CF}=\dfrac{3-(-6)}{5-8}=-3$。

C. 【答案】 $(-3，26)$

【解析】

天璇　　天樞　　　　　　　　　　　　北
$(9，8)$　$(7，11)$　　　　　5　　　　　A
　　　　1

$(7，11)=\dfrac{5(9，8)+A}{1+5}$

$\Rightarrow A=6(7，11)-5(9，8)=(-3，26)$。

D. 【答案】 $x=-1$ 時，最小值為 -3。

【解析】 設 $C(2t，2t^2)$，$\overrightarrow{AB}=(6，6)$，

$\overrightarrow{AC}=(2t+2，2t^2-2)$

$\overrightarrow{AB}\cdot\overrightarrow{AC}=12t+12+12t^2-12=12(t+\dfrac{1}{2})^2-3$

當 $x=2t=-1$ 時，$min=-3$。

E. 【答案】 7

　　【解析】 $APQR = \triangle ABC - \triangle PBQ - \triangle RCQ$

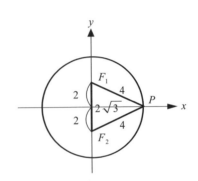

$$\Rightarrow 20\sqrt{3} = \frac{\sqrt{3}}{4}(13^2 - x^2 - (x-13)^2)$$

$$\Rightarrow (x-5)(x-8) = 0$$

$$\Rightarrow 取 x = 5$$

則 $\overline{PR} = \sqrt{5^2 + 8^2 - 2 \cdot 5 \cdot 8 \cdot cos\,60°} = 7$。

F. 【答案】 $m = 12$，$n = 16$

　　【解析】 $2a = 4 + 4 = 8$

$$\Rightarrow a = 4，b = 2\sqrt{3}$$

∵ 此橢圓為直橢

∴ $m = b^2 = 12$，$n = a^2 = 16$

G. 【答案】 $\dfrac{3}{7}$

　　【解析】 3 邊長為 $a = \dfrac{14}{13} - \dfrac{1}{13} = 1$，$b = 1 - (-1) = 2$，

$$c = -1 - (-4) = 3$$

對角線長分別為 $\sqrt{3^2 + 2^2}$ 、 $\sqrt{3^2 + 1^2}$ 、 $\sqrt{1^2 + 2^2 + 3^2}$

$$\Rightarrow 機率 = \frac{4 + 4 + 4}{C_2^8 = 28} = \frac{3}{7}$$

101 年大學入學學科能力測驗試題 社會考科

單選題 (佔 144 分)

說明： 第 1 題至第 72 題皆計分。每題有 4 個選項，其中只有一個是最正確或最適當的選項，請畫記在答案卡之「選擇題答案區」。各題答對者，得 2 分；答錯、未作答或畫記多於一個選項者，該題以零分計算。

1. 某工會發動罷工爭取薪資福利調整，小明認爲自己沒有參與罷工的必要，反正罷工成功自己也可以享受加薪，萬一罷工失敗，因爲自己沒參加，也不會影響到飯碗。下列何者最適合解釋小明的行爲？
   (A) 自願性不足
   (B) 公德心缺乏
   (C) 搭便車心態
   (D) 次文化影響

2. 學者研究某縣市兩個地理範圍與人口數量、性別等特性相近的社區，其社區營造的成果如表一。對於甲乙兩社區之社區營造的描述，下列何者最爲正確？

表一

社區營造項目	甲社區	乙社區
居民可說出自己社區名稱的比例	14 %	75 %
過去一年社區新增公共建設的金額	180 萬元	90 萬元
過去一年社區活動的平均參與人次	20 人次	193 人次
過去一年社區獲得政府補助活動的金額	85 萬元	50 萬元

   (A) 甲社區的營造成果較乙社區來得優越
   (B) 甲社區較乙社區更具備社區自治精神
   (C) 乙社區的社區認同意識較甲社區爲高
   (D) 乙社區較甲社區更需要政府指導協助

3. 「女性占所有管理及經理職位比率」及「女性占國會議員席次比率」二者可做為觀察女性政經參與及其對決策影響程度的重要指標。表二為三個國家在這二項指標的數據。

表二

國別	甲		乙		丙	
年度	1989	2009	1989	2009	1989	2009
女性占所有管理及經理職位比率（％）	12.0	25.9	17.6	37.3	6.6	10.1
女性占國會議員席次比率（％）	8.9	24.5	13.7	28.3	4.8	9.2

依據上表，將這三個國家的性別不平等程度由高到低加以排列，下列何者正確？

(A) 甲乙丙　　　(B) 甲丙乙　　　(C) 乙甲丙　　　(D) 丙甲乙

4. 我國為確保原住民的基本權益，於民國94 年制定並施行《原住民族基本法》，這是下列何種主張的具體表現？

(A) 文明進化　　　　　　　(B) 多元文化

(C) 族群同化　　　　　　　(D) 我族中心

5. 「民主政治」是普世潮流，因為它對人權的保護有所提昇，且對人民的需求有所回應，而「非民主政治」則不然。若我們想要了解某國的政治概況，可以根據下列哪種作為來判斷其為「非民主政治」國家？

(A) 對政黨政治的競爭規則進行規範

(B) 對國內媒體與政治言論進行管控

(C) 必要時宣布國家進入緊急狀態限制某些自由

(D) 嚴格執行國家之法律，沒有商議妥協的餘地

6. 我國某市議會三讀通過該市公共場所母乳哺育自治條例：婦女即使出門在外，也可在公共場所為嬰幼兒哺育母乳，任何人不得有制止、驅離或其他影響哺育的行為。次年，中央政府也跟進對婦女在公共場所哺育母乳立法，並公布全國施行。關於當時該市率先制定有關公共場所哺育母乳的條例，下列敘述何者正確？

    (A) 此條例制定落實地方分權的精神

    (B) 此條例凸顯中央與地方政府的權責不明

    (C) 此自治條例仍須經立法院同意始能生效

    (D) 該市無權制定此條例，故中央於次年統一立法

7. 依照目前臺海兩岸的現況，對我國而言，出現領土及統治權之落差。按我國現行憲法，以下敘述何者正確？

    (A) 我國目前統治權所及地區，憲法上稱為「中華臺北」

    (B) 我國目前統治權所及地區，憲法上稱為「中華民國臺灣省」

    (C) 我國領土除臺、澎、金、馬以外之地區，憲法上稱為「內地」

    (D) 我國領土除臺、澎、金、馬以外之地區，憲法上稱為「大陸地區」

8. 公民投票是民主政治中為實現「主權在民」而有的一種制度設計。以下有關我國舉辦公民投票的敘述何者正確？

    (A) 公民投票的成本很高，故我國規定每四年舉辦一次

    (B) 我國曾對「是否加入聯合國」及「是否重返聯合國」舉辦公民投票

    (C) 我國舉辦公民投票乃因它是一般民主國家制定公共政策最常用的方式

    (D) 我國曾對是否與大陸簽訂ECFA（兩岸經濟合作架構協定）案舉辦公民投票

9. 某內閣制國家的國會議員共有一百席,1991 年到 2004 年共進行了六次國會大選,選後席次分配如圖一。請問該國比較接近下列哪種政黨體系?

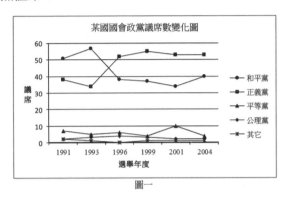

圖一

(A) 兩黨制　　(B) 多黨制　　(C) 一黨專政制　　(D) 一黨獨大制

10. 吐瓦魯(Tuvalu)是一個隨時會被海水淹沒的迷你島國,在這裡協助觀光行銷的臺灣志工林小姐說:「想趁著年輕,到處走走看看。」所以選擇出國擔任志工,並體驗到什麼叫做「窮得只剩下快樂」。若以經濟學中個人選擇的觀點來看,下列敘述何者正確?
(A) 年輕稍縱即逝,青春是有限的資源
(B) 賺錢的機會多得是,錢財並不具有稀少性
(C) 當志工僅能收取少數或甚至不收取報酬,對社會貢獻有限
(D) 「想趁著年輕,到處走走看看。」說明遊覽各國是當志工的機會成本

11. 由於瓶裝水具有極大的便利性,全球瓶裝水的消費迅速增加,購買進口瓶裝水也成了時髦的象徵。但瓶裝水的消費及運送引發了環境問題,近年來社運人士陸續發起「反瓶裝水運動」。依上述有關瓶裝水所引發的問題,下列敘述何者最為正確?
(A) 瓶裝水是造成水資源污染的主要原因
(B) 瓶裝水需求增加,極可能造成水資源的耗竭

(C) 瓶裝水的包裝及運送大量排碳，助長溫室效應

(D) 國際間水資源短缺，各國的水資源戰爭一觸即發

12. 李媽媽在夜市租了一個店面開設小吃店，她由家裡搬來 1 套桌椅，並添購 5 套桌椅。每個週末，她在大學讀企業管理的兒子也會到店裡幫忙。請問下列有關生產要素的敘述，哪項是正確的？
(A) 所承租的店面屬於土地
(B) 由家裡搬來的桌椅屬於資本
(C) 李媽媽對小吃口味的更新屬於勞動
(D) 李媽媽的兒子週末付出的時間屬於企業能力

13. 某工廠發生爆炸事件，衍生成地方抗爭，凸顯出經濟發展與永續發展的衝突現象，而最後當地政府雖與該工廠達成高額賠償金的共識，仍無法獲得當地居民的認同。請問以下有關此問題的敘述何者正確？
(A) 此爆炸事件反映出共有財的悲歌（ Tragedy of the Commons ）問題
(B) 由於雙方對爆炸原因認定不一，此乃資訊不完全而衍生之供需失衡現象
(C) 此乃該工廠與當地居民對於爆炸所造成的外部成本之影響認知不同所致
(D) 這是私有財產權界定不明確所致，透過政府的介入與立法規範即可解決

14. 我國影片在國內整體電影票房的占有率長期偏低。雖說電影發展的好壞與票房占有率並無直接對等關係，國內是否要採行保護政策亦多所爭議，但僅就經濟邏輯來看，不考量觀眾的偏好、所得等其他條件，請問下列何種政策最有可能提高我國影片的國內票房占有率？

(A) 調降隨電影票課徵之娛樂稅

(B) 對外國影片之進口採配額限制

(C) 加強盜版影片的查緝，並加重處罰

(D) 與外國簽署協定，增進雙方電影貿易

15. 某大學男女學生十人，為抗議該校調漲學費，相約於中午12 點
在學校操場集合，持空碗，扮乞丐，遊行校園一周；行動途中還
舉起抗議海報，呼喊口號，表達心中不滿。這些大學生的抗議行
為本身是在行使憲法所保障的何種基本權利？

(A) 結社自由　　　　　　(B) 受教育權

(C) 人身自由　　　　　　(D) 言論自由

16. 某員警進行巡查時，隨機攔檢機車騎士，並要求出示證件。有騎
士不願接受盤查，大聲咆哮；員警先拉其下車，再以擒拿術壓
制，限制行動，最後將之帶回警局訊問。該員警執行職務的行為
違反下列哪項法治國基本原則？

(A) 比例原則　　　　　　(B) 平等原則

(C) 行政中立原則　　　　(D) 信賴保護原則

17. 小偷在竊取路邊車輛的音響時，被巡邏員警逮個正著，並帶回警
局訊問。關於接下來的刑事法律程序，下列敘述何者正確？

(A) 警察機關訊問完畢後可以移送法院，並提起公訴

(B) 起訴後，警察機關可以拘留行竊者等候法院審理

(C) 行竊者在警局接受訊問時可以要求聘請律師在場

(D) 遭竊者可依《犯罪被害人保護法》要求政府補償

18. 民法上所稱的行為能力是指當事人能夠獨立為有效法律行為的能
力，例如：獨立與他人成立買賣契約。下列有關行為能力的敘
述，何者正確？

(A) 年滿十八歲爲民法上之成年人，有完全行爲能力

(B) 剛滿十歲的國小三年級學生，因未達十四歲，故無行爲能力

(C) 剛滿十四歲之人，得不經法定代理人允許，購買考試用參考書

(D) 男滿十六歲即可與他人爲有效的結婚行爲，毋需法定代理人同意

19. 一群勞工因爲勞資糾紛協商不成，因此申請集會遊行上街抗議，街旁某唱片行則大聲播放歌曲支持這群勞工。執勤的警察分局長認爲唱片行的做法有礙秩序，即率員警進入店內，拉下鐵門，並取走音響裡的 CD 光碟，告誡店家後率隊離去。關於此事件，以下敘述何者正確？

(A) 警察取走 CD 光碟是爲維護社會秩序，符合法治國原則的要求

(B) 唱片行大聲播放歌曲，表達對抗議群衆的支持，屬於人身自由的展現

(C) 如果警察分局長是在檢察官的指揮下率隊進入店家，就是合法的執行職務行爲

(D) 警察進入店家並取走 CD 光碟是一種搜索扣押，應取得法院核發的搜索票才算合法

20. 某校 21 歲的張生經常受到陳生欺凌。陳生後來要求張生參加黑道喪禮，張生不願，陳生警告他到時不去就要把他「埋了」！張生忍無可忍，動手砍殺陳生。對於這個法律事件，下列分析何者不正確？

(A) 張生是具有完全責任能力之人

(B) 法院判決時不必考慮張生所受的委屈

(C) 張生雖然遭受委屈，但他的殺人行爲仍不被法律允許

(D) 本案顯示：犯罪的成因可能很複雜，不一定可以把責任完全歸給行爲人

21-22 為題組

◎ 我國政府制定《特種貨物及勞務稅條例》（即是俗稱的「奢侈稅」），從民國 100 年 6 月起實施，其中一個目的是希望能夠壓低近年來不斷上漲的房價，尤其是針對交通便利的都會地區。

21. 按照現代民主理論，我國課徵「奢侈稅」的作法可說是符合了「國家的目的與功能」中的「落實社會正義」這一項目。以下何者是這種論點的最主要理由？
    (A) 一個正義的社會，不應存在奢侈的消費行為
    (B) 都會地區房價若是下降，可改善城鄉區域發展的差距
    (C) 傳統上認為節儉是美德，所以政府有責任導正人民消費習慣
    (D) 民主政府應照顧人民的福祉及基本生活需求，包括居住的權利

22. 假設「奢侈稅」造成買方預期豪宅價格將下跌，導致市場需求減少，賣方因政策的衝擊而不願將豪宅賣出，造成市場供給減少；請問在這樣的情況下，豪宅的市場均衡價格與均衡數量會如何變動？
    (A) 價格一定下跌，但數量不一定增加
    (B) 數量一定減少，但價格不一定提高
    (C) 價格一定上漲，但數量不一定減少
    (D) 數量一定增加，但價格不一定降低

23-24 為題組

◎ 某國為了解年輕人結婚意願與生育率變低的原因，其研究機構調查 20 至 39 歲民眾對婚姻的態度（如圖二）。圖中數據顯示，有結婚意願的男性與女性中，尚未結婚的原因主要有「沒有經濟基礎」與「尚無合適對象」兩個理由。

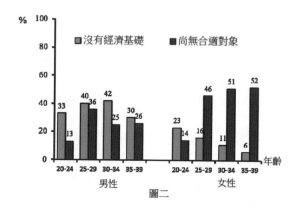

圖二

23. 根據圖中數據，下列敘述何者<u>最不合理</u>？
    (A) 很多未婚男性認為養家是男人的責任
    (B) 經濟條件不是影響某國年輕人結婚意願的唯一因素
    (C) 對未婚女性而言，年紀愈輕，結婚意願愈不易受到經濟壓力的影響
    (D) 就未婚男性而言，其結婚意願受到無合適對象的影響較女性來得小

24. 如果政府為了鼓勵民眾提高結婚與生育意願，推動平價社會住宅、生育補貼、公辦幼兒托育及減免國小學童學費等政策。請問圖中哪群人的結婚意願最可能受這些政策影響？
    (A) 30 至 34 歲的未婚男性　　(B) 25 至 29 歲的未婚女性
    (C) 35 至 39 歲的未婚男性　　(D) 20 至 24 歲的未婚女性

25. 一位民意代表主張：「今日臺灣發電條件豐富，政府應研究鐵路電氣化的可能性，其經濟效益可提高人民所得。」主管交通的官員答覆：「關於鐵路電氣化問題，美援會研究認為需再慎重，本案中央繼續研究中。」這位民意代表最可能是：
    (A) 1930 年代，街庄協議會的議員
    (B) 1960 年代，臺灣省議會的議員

(C) 1980 年代，立法院的立法委員

(D) 1990 年代，國會中的國大代表

26. 春秋晚期，鄭國的執政大夫子產將刑法鑄於銅鼎，公布法律條文使國人周知。此舉引發鄰近晉國貴族之疑慮，認爲人民可有成文法律做爲靠山，據此爭取自身權益，極可能威脅既有的社會穩定及政治秩序。子產的改革與晉國貴族的疑慮，可以說明當時社會的哪種現象？

(A) 平民興起漸成爲國家中堅力量

(B) 政府的行政權萎縮， 民權增強

(C) 貴族立法鎭壓百姓以維護封建

(D) 司法解釋與裁量改由人民主導

27. 歷史上某一時期，甲乙雙方舉行效忠儀式：甲方向乙方保證，願以自由人身分，終身服事乙方，絕不脫離乙方保護，如有違背，願以金錢賠償；乙方則保證，宣誓之後，將終身保護甲方。這個效忠儀式最可能在何時何處舉行？

(A) 八世紀前期君士坦丁堡的皇宮

(B) 十二世紀中期法國北部的莊園

(C) 十六世紀後期英國南部的城堡

(D) 十九世紀後期美國南部的棉田

28. 媒體報導：「波蘭國會於本月中通過加入北大西洋公約組織（簡稱北約）案，波蘭預定在三月間與捷克及匈牙利同時成爲北約新會員。」這則報導出現的時代背景爲何？

(A) 二戰結束時，美蘇兩國在東歐對峙，美國拉攏波、捷等國加入北約

(B) 韓戰結束後，法國欲擴大在歐洲勢力，企圖說服東歐各國加入北約

(C) 越戰爆發時，西歐欲打擊華沙公約組織，勸說波、捷等國加入北約

(D) 蘇聯解體後，東歐向西方靠攏，波、捷、匈牙利等國家欲加入北約

29. 一位作家呼籲：希望作家不要身處危難，卻仍然成天做著新式或舊式的鴛鴦蝴蝶夢。我們要關心現實，寫我們的現實，主要一點便是反買辦、反崇洋媚外、反分裂的地方主義。這段話反映哪個時期臺灣的文學思潮？

(A) 1950 年代的反共文學　　(B) 1960 年代的現代文學

(C) 1970 年代的鄉土文學　　(D) 1980 年代的浪漫文學

30. 某個帝國，在十一世紀初是歐洲最強盛的國家，十四世紀以後，境內諸侯紛紛追求自身利益，互相攻伐，國勢漸衰。十七世紀，又因宗教問題，造成內部分裂。十九世紀初，帝國甚至遭拿破崙解散。這個帝國是指：

(A) 俄羅斯帝國　　　　　　(B) 拜占庭帝國

(C) 神聖羅馬帝國　　　　　(D) 鄂圖曼帝國

31. 十六世紀起，歐亞間的海上貿易興起，許多歐洲國家紛紛前來亞洲經商。歐洲某國王室出資組成船隊，前往印度與東亞地區貿易。國王為反制抗議教派，避免其擴張，還願與教廷合作，免費將傳教士送往商船所到之處傳教。這位國王是：

(A) 西班牙國王菲利普　　　(B) 英格蘭王伊莉莎白

(C) 俄國皇帝彼得大帝　　　(D) 瑞典國王古斯塔夫

32. 一篇論文裡的關鍵詞有：中日關係、山東問題、胡適、巴黎和會。這篇論文討論的主題最可能是：

(A) 庚子拳亂　　　　　　　(B) 五四運動

(C) 瀋陽事變　　　　　　　(D) 七七事變

33. 一位商人自述：家中原本頗有積蓄，曾經擁有一家運輸公司。後因為投資股票，一夜之間，家財全部化為烏有。他為了養家活口，只得到碼頭當搬運工，但工作並不固定，收入有限。許多朋友則因無法繳付房貸，住家遭銀行查封，只得跟許多人一起在公園搭帳棚，領失業救濟金，不相信政府能解決他們的困境。

這種情形最可能是：
(A) 1800 年拿破崙戰爭後的巴黎
(B) 1918 年第一次大戰後的倫敦
(C) 1932 年經濟蕭條時期的紐約
(D) 1950 年第二次大戰後的上海

34. 臺灣原本不產耕牛，主政者在南北兩路各設「牛頭司」，負責引進牛隻繁殖，以用於耕作。主政者並在各地修築水利設施，提供耕牛、農具與種籽；又大量招募「中土遺民」前來開墾。這是何時的情況？
(A) 荷蘭時期
(B) 清領初期
(C) 日治時期
(D) 戰後初期

35. 某一時期，立國的理念是：「國家應由受過良好教育、擁有財產的人來管理；他們可以制訂法律，保護人民財產，維持社會安寧。人民應當遵守法律、熱愛國家。」所有法律也都依據這樣的理念制訂。這應當是下列哪個時期的觀念？
(A) 秦始皇統一六國時期的法家思想
(B) 拜占庭帝國查士丁尼法典的主張
(C) 英格蘭王約翰簽署大憲章的概念
(D) 法蘭西帝國拿破崙法典立法精神

36. 學者指出：某個時期的農村市鎮主要分布在黃河中、下游和長江三角洲；黃河中、下游的市鎮數量很多，但每個市鎮的貿易額卻

不大；長江三角洲的情況恰好相反，市鎮數量少，但每個市鎮的貿易額都很大。不過，政府在兩個地區所收的商業稅大致相等。這種經濟現象最可能出現於何時？

(A) 唐代前期，江南地區漸次開發

(B) 北宋時期，商業繁榮市鎮興起

(C) 蒙元時期，華北經濟漸趨沒落

(D) 明代時期，江南市鎮經濟擴大

37. 日本軍方在一份布告書中說：「我軍所向，蕃人懾服。」但當要與清國議和之際，清國政府生出異議，未能立刻達成和議。「現在，兩國商議已決，即將接受清國請求而撤軍，並將該地人民交還清國。」這份布告書應當是：

(A) 牡丹社事件後日軍的公告

(B) 日軍佔領琉球之後的公告

(C) 甲午戰後日軍對臺的公告

(D) 日俄戰爭期間對東北公告

38. 一位官員指出：為紓緩市場銅錢不足問題，政府應當禁止民間鑄造銅器。經大臣討論後，向皇帝建議：除銅鏡之外，禁止民間以銅為原料，鑄造器物。此事最可能發生於：

(A) 秦朝，統一六國後，為促進商業活動，鼓勵民間自鑄銅錢

(B) 西晉，因漢末大亂後，百廢待舉，政府希望擴大銅錢流通

(C) 晚唐，因商業漸繁榮，貨幣不足，必須確保銅錢供應充足

(D) 清中期，因白銀流失日趨嚴重，朝廷下令，擴大銅錢流通

39. 古董商販售一批聲稱是從河南安陽出土的甲骨文書，指出：這批書寫於牛肩胛骨的文物，主要內容為土地交易契約。幾位同學發表看法，下列何種說法最可信？

(A) 這批文物從河南安陽出土，又有甲骨文書，應當是眞品

(B) 刻寫在牛肩胛骨，而非書寫在龜甲，故極有可能爲贋品

(C) 甲骨文直到清末才出土，無法僞造，這批文物應爲眞品

(D) 商代並無土地交易行爲，自然不可能有契約，應爲贋品

40. 一位統治者自述其生平事蹟：「19 歲那年，國家受到奸黨蹂躪，是我招募軍隊，打敗奸黨，才重建和平。元老院選我爲執政官，控制所有權力，但我拒絕獨裁，不僅恢復了許多逐漸沒落的傳統，也爲後代子孫立下許多典範。」這位統治者最可能是：

(A) 亞歷山大大帝　　　　　(B) 羅馬將領凱撒

(C) 羅馬皇帝屋大維　　　　(D) 羅馬皇帝君士坦丁

41. 一首詩描述古埃及的農業生活，提到以下特徵：甲、尼羅河定期氾濫，使埃及生生不息；乙、河水澆灌了沙漠，養育肥美魚類；丙、河岸有牲畜覓食；丁、神廟定期舉行豐年慶典。上述哪項特徵最足以說明此詩所描述的是農業定耕生活方式？

(A) 甲　　　　(B) 乙　　　　(C) 丙　　　　(D) 丁

42. 十九世紀中期，一位俄國學者批評政府的某項政策，認爲它「改變數百年習慣的生活方式，摧毀自古以來人民與土地的連結關係。」因此他呼籲：「讓我們根據傳統的原則，重新恢復國家與人民、人民與土地之關係。」這位學者批評的政策爲何？

(A) 解放農奴　　(B) 組織公社　　(C) 農地重劃　　(D) 土地國有

43. 一張老相片顯示：火車站中有數列滿載士兵的火車，其中有兩列預計開赴比利時前線，另有一列即將駛往東方邊界，車廂上的標語寫著：「向沙俄宣戰！爲祖國奮鬥！」這張相片最可能是何時的情景？

(A) 1854 年的克里米亞戰爭爆發後,英軍開往前線

(B) 1870 年德法戰爭爆發,德意志聯軍向法國開拔

(C) 1914 年,第一次世界大戰爆發,德軍準備出發

(D) 1939 年歐洲大戰爆發,德軍準備進攻蘇聯之際

44. 自某個時期起,藝術創作強調恢復希臘與羅馬的傳統,藝術家精研人體結構,重視透視法。他們的地位大幅提昇,非以往的工匠可比,貴族與富商都願意收購藝術作品珍藏。這個時期最可能是:

(A) 西元十二世紀   (B) 西元十五世紀

(C) 西元十八世紀   (D) 西元十九世紀

45. 一份臺灣的考古報告記載:其居民主要住在水岸的稍高階地,已形成定居的小型聚落。他們使用石製的生產工具,如石鋤、石斧,種植根莖類的作物。這一文化分布地區廣及中國的閩南和廣東沿海。此文化遺址最可能是:

(A) 長濱文化   (B) 網形文化

(C) 大坌坑文化   (D) 十三行文化

46. 近世臺灣開發以來,逐漸形成「大租戶—小租戶—佃戶」的土地所有與經營結構。某個時期,政府為了解決財政不足的問題,除了清查全臺土地,防止逃漏稅外,更以行政命令,剝奪某個層級地主的土地所有權,而以政府發行的公債以及現金作為補償。如此一來,政府得以向直接經營土地者徵稅,擴大徵稅對象,稅收也得以增加。這次土地所有權的變動最可能是指:

(A) 鄭成功實施屯田制   (B) 劉銘傳行減四留六法

(C) 日本取消了大租權   (D) 民國政府三七五減租

47. 西方商人到中國貿易時,地方政府常藉各種名義收取費用,令商人不勝其擾。在一場戰爭後,中國政府同意各國商品除繳交 5%

的進口關稅外，不用再繳納任何雜費。從此以後，各國貨物正式
繳稅進口，到各處販賣。這場戰爭是：
(A) 鴉片戰爭　　(B) 英法聯軍　　(C) 甲午戰爭　　(D) 八國聯軍

48. 「現代化的關鍵在於發展科技。我們不可能光靠空談變成現代國
家，我們國內的科技、教育都比附近國家落後 20 年，我們需要
有知識、有訓練的人才，就好像當初的日本。不過他們是靠新興
起的資產階級，我們要靠普羅大眾。我相信我們一定會做得比日
本好。」這種說法最可能出現於：
(A) 1890 年代的俄國　　　　(B) 1930 年代的德國
(C) 1950 年代的印度　　　　(D) 1980 年代的中國

49. 某企業於 1972 年在臺灣設廠，並成立研發部門。1992 年以後，
陸續在江蘇（1992）、上海（1994）、荷蘭（1996）和四川
（2004）設廠。江蘇、上海和四川廠的產品，多在該地銷售或
外銷東南亞；荷蘭廠和臺灣廠的產品，多在歐洲銷售。下列哪個
概念最足以說明該企業在各地設廠的過程？
(A) 工業慣性　　(B) 區位擴散　　(C) 區位聚集　　(D) 空間移轉

50. 臺灣曾文溪出海口附近，每年 9 月底有許多黑面琵鷺從北方陸續
飛來，在潟湖區過冬覓食，次年 3 月再陸續飛返北方。某同學觀
察黑面琵鷺的生態習性，並結合國內、外觀察紀錄，在無電腦製
圖工具協助下，欲繪製黑面琵鷺年中遷徙路線圖。下列哪項地理
科的學習成就，最有助於該同學完成遷徙路線圖？
(A) 了解地圖的座標系統
(B) 認識大比例尺地形圖的圖例
(C) 利用等高線判斷各種地形的技能
(D) 區分空間資料和屬性資料的差異

51. 圖三是世界貿易組織（WTO）公布的 1950-2004 年間四個時期，全球總貿易額和總生產值的平均年增加率圖。下列何者最能用來解讀圖三所顯示的資訊？

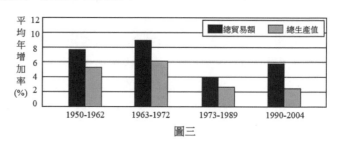

圖三

(A) 全球分工盛行，使區域間相互依賴增強
(B) 產品生命週期縮短，導致工業區位移轉
(C) 工業區老化，引起區域經濟結構再調整
(D) 新興資本市場興起，跨國社會空間出現

52-53 為題組

◎ 馬利、尼日、查德、塞內加爾和布吉納法索等非洲國家，以經濟作物的出口為主要外匯來源。長期以來，經濟作物出口價格變動不大，但是進口糧食、工業產品卻越來越多，價格也節節高漲。為了平衡貿易赤字，這些國家以擴大經濟作物種植面積為主要政策，以致傳統農業土地利用改變。請問：

52. 從五國的環境特性判斷，其創造外匯的主體是下列哪組經濟作物？
(A) 油棕、可可　　　　　(B) 棉花、花生
(C) 甘蔗、茶葉　　　　　(D) 橡膠、香蕉

53. 該五國以經濟作物的產品出口創造外匯，利用外匯進口糧食和工業產品的現象，最適合用下列哪個概念解釋？
(A) 物流　　　　　　　　(B) 三角貿易
(C) 空間分工鏈　　　　　(D) 殖民地式經濟

<u>54-56 爲題組</u>

◎ 表三是 2006 年中國一些經濟指標和原物料消耗占世界的比例。伴
　隨經濟發展而來的是環境問題嚴重和都市化程度迅速上升。如沙
　塵暴發生頻率逐年增加，空氣汙染物排放量已居世界前茅，且對
　全球環境影響日劇。2006 年，把在都市生活半年以上的農村流動
　人口也歸類爲都市人口時，中國都市化程度爲 43.9%，但其中至
　少有 1.2 億人在制度、社會地位及一些生活與文化層面，無法過
　實質的都市生活。若扣除這部分人口，中國都市化程度可能就只
　剩 33% 左右。請問：

表三

經濟指標	項目	占世界 (%)	原物料消耗	項目	占世界 (%)
	GDP	5.5		能源	15.0
	出口額	8.0		鋼	30.0
	進口額	6.4		水泥	45.0

54. 中國經濟指標與原物料消耗占世界比例的數據差異，最能反映中
　　國的下列哪項特色？
　　(A) 人口數量多且分布不均　　(B) 作爲世界工廠色彩濃厚
　　(C) 區域貧富差距相當嚴重　　(D) 經濟特區發展速度減緩

55. 中國發生的沙塵暴和排放的空氣汙染物，在下列哪個時段最易影
　　響到臺灣？
　　(A) 初春－仲夏（ 3－7月）　(B) 仲夏－初冬（ 7－12月）
　　(C) 晚秋－初春（ 11－3月）(D) 仲冬－初夏（ 1－6月）

56. 中國都市化程度雖已達43.9%，但有許多都市人口仍無法實質享
　　受都市生活帶來的便利，主要受哪項因素的影響？
　　(A) 都市階層體系的發展　　(B) 推拉因素與供需互補
　　(C) 都市土地利用的分區　　(D) 人口的城鄉分隔制度

57-58 為題組

◎ 表四為 2010 年全球六大地區國外旅客到訪人數與觀光外匯收入資料表。請問：

表四

地區	到訪人數		地區	觀光外匯收入	
	百萬人	%		十億美元	%
歐洲	476.6	50.7	歐洲	406.2	44.7
亞太	203.8	21.7	亞太	248.7	27.4
北美洲	98.2	10.4	北美洲	131.2	14.4
中南美洲	51.5	5.5	中南美洲	51.0	5.6
漠南非洲	30.7	3.3	漠南非洲	21.6	2.4
西亞和北非	79.0	8.4	西亞和北非	50.3	5.5
全球	939.8	100.0	全球	909.0	100.0

57. 若要比較各地區國外旅客到訪人數，較適合採用下列哪些統計圖來展示？甲、曲線圖；乙、長條圖；丙、圓餅圖；丁、等值線圖。
(A) 甲乙　　　　　　　(B) 甲丁　　(C) 乙丙　　(D) 丙丁

58. 從表四判斷，觀光遊憩業最發達的地區主要集中在下列哪兩種氣候區內？
(A) 溫帶季風氣候區、溫帶草原氣候區
(B) 熱帶雨林氣候區、熱帶莽原氣候區
(C) 熱帶季風氣候區、熱帶沙漠氣候區
(D) 溫帶海洋性氣候區、溫帶地中海型氣候區

59-60 為題組

◎ 表五是臺灣四個國家風景區到訪遊客人數及其季節分配資料表。請問：

表五

國家風景區		冬 (12-2月)	春 (3-5月)	夏 (6-8月)	秋 (9-11月)	合計
甲	人數	48813	475063	985656	240808	1750340
	%	2.79	27.14	56.31	13.76	100.00
乙	人數	3485	10765	23607	16151	54008
	%	6.45	19.93	43.71	29.90	100.00
丙	人數	2347455	2817534	2396048	1579340	9140377
	%	25.68	30.83	26.21	17.28	100.00
丁	人數	382736	337170	295243	302571	1317720
	%	29.05	25.59	22.41	22.96	100.00

59. 若將「觀光遊憩業商圈」定義為「遊憩資源的遊客來源範圍」，
　　則表五中哪個國家風景區的商圈可能最大？
　　(A) 甲　　　　(B) 乙　　　　(C) 丙　　　　(D) 丁

60. 哪兩個國家風景區最可能位於離島地區？
　　(A) 甲乙　　　(B) 甲丁　　　(C) 乙丙　　　(D) 丙丁

61-63 為題組

◎ 中南美洲地形相當多樣，大致可以分為平原、山地、盆地、高原
　等地形區。有些地區地質古老，有些地區火山活動頻繁，金屬礦
　物資源豐富。牧業發達，農業以栽培經濟作物為主，種類繁多。大
　部分國家都市化程度很高，但首要型的都市體系型態顯著。請問：

61. 該大洲的金屬礦物資源，主要分布在哪兩種地形區？
　　(A) 平原、山地　　　　　　(B) 山地、高原
　　(C) 盆地、高原　　　　　　(D) 平原、盆地

62. 該大洲某地區的主要經濟作物有葡萄、柑橘、橄欖、無花果等。
　　該地區最可能位於哪個國家？
　　(A) 智利　　　(B) 烏拉圭　　(C) 墨西哥　　(D) 玻利維亞

63. 「大部分國家都市化程度很高，但首要型的都市體系型態顯著。」
   這種現象與下列該大洲哪項區域特色的關聯性最密切？
   (A) 高地都市眾多　　　　　　　(B) 貧富不均顯著
   (C) 區域結盟緊密　　　　　　　(D) 多元文化熔爐

64-66 為題組

◎ 圖四是某同學在進行「鄉
   土地理專題研究」時，使
   用網路地理資訊系統製作
   的交通路線圖。請問：

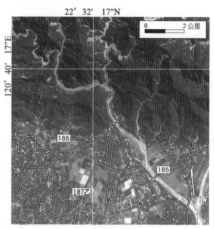

圖四

64. GIS 的空間資料模式可分
   為向量式和網格式，圖四
   的圖形原始資料中，何者
   屬於網格式資料？
   (A) 比例尺　　　(B) 經緯線
   (C) 衛星影像　　(D) 道路系統

65. 圖四所在地區僅就其氣候類型而言，最宜規畫發展下列哪種商業
   性農業活動？
   (A) 放牧業　　　　　　　　　　(B) 混合農業
   (C) 熱帶栽培業　　　　　　　　(D) 商業性穀物農業

66. 圖五（見第 14 頁下半部）是四個地區的數值立體地形圖。何者
   最能展示圖四的地形實況？
   (A) 甲　　　　　(B) 乙　　　　　(C) 丙　　　　　(D) 丁

67-69 為題組

◎ 聯合國歷年發布的「人類發展程度指標（HDI）」，是用來衡量
   各國的發展水準。表六是四個國家2010 年人口密度、HDI 及一些
   社會指標資料。請問：

表六

國家	人口密度(人/km²)	HDI	平均壽命	性別比	國民平均就學年數	老年人口比例(%)
甲	403	0.385	51.1	96.4	3.3	2.98
乙	126	0.385	54.6	100.1	4.3	3.41
丙	111	0.719	76.9	100.3	10.4	11.04
丁	8	0.719	67.2	86.1	8.8	15.26

67. 表中哪兩個國家的都市化程度較低？
    (A) 甲乙　　　(B) 甲丁　　　(C) 乙丙　　　(D) 丙丁

68. 就人口轉型過程的四個階段而言，表中哪兩個國家最可能已經進入「低穩定階段」？
    (A) 甲乙　　　(B) 甲丁　　　(C) 乙丙　　　(D) 丙丁

69. 表中四個國家的平均每人國民生產毛額，若按HDI 的概念來推估，則從高到低的排列順序為何？
    (A) 甲丁丙乙　　(B) 乙丁甲丙　　(C) 丙丁甲乙　　(D) 丁丙甲乙

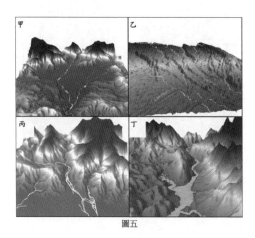

圖五

70-72 爲題組

◎ 照片一（見本頁下半部）是臺灣公路系統上的四個路標。請問：

70. 就臺灣公路系統編號慣例，單數表示公路起迄點的相對位置爲南北向。四個路標所顯示的四條南北向公路路線，其中哪一條最可能位於中央山脈與海岸山脈之間？

(A) 臺 1 線　　(B) 臺 3 線　　(C) 臺 9 線　　(D) 臺 61 線

71. 就臺灣四大區域而言，哪個「路標座落的地點」所屬區域是臺灣最重要的蔬菜和花卉等農產品供應地？

(A) 甲　　　　(B) 乙　　　　(C) 丙　　　　(D) 丁

72. 這四個「路標座落的地點」，由低緯往高緯的排列順序爲何？

(A) 甲乙丙丁　　　　　　　(B) 甲丙丁乙

(C) 乙甲丙丁　　　　　　　(D) 丁丙乙甲

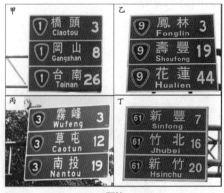

照片一

101年度學科能力測驗社會科試題詳解

單選題

1. **C**

   【解析】 依題意『小明認為自己沒有參與罷工的必要，假若罷工成功自己也可以享受加薪』，此即所謂『搭便車』的行為，意即沒有付出貢獻，但卻獲得其他團體所努力的成果。

2. **C**

   【解析】 社區營造成功的關鍵並非經費的多寡或政府補助的程度，關鍵在於是否建立起『社區意識』，也就是居民對居住社區具有認同感與歸屬感，並願意主動參與社區內公共事務的意識。

3. **D**

   【解析】 由 1989～2009 年兩項數據中，增加幅度最小的國家，表示該國性別不平等程度較高，反之較低，所以依據以下數據丙國最不平等、甲國次之、乙國最平等。

國度	丙	甲	乙
年度	1989～2009 增加幅度		
女性占所有管理及經理職位比率 (%)	3.5	13.9	19.7
女性占國會議員席次比率 (%)	4.4	15.6	14.6

4. **B**

【解析】 多元文化的精神，即指尊重與認同不同於自己文化的概念，過去政府對於原住民族多採取同化政策，因而使得原住民族的文化日漸流失，而近年來政府開始關注多元文化的重要，遂制定《原住民族基本法》以保存並維護 原住民族的文化權。

5. **B**

【解析】 所謂「非民主政治」，執政者為鞏固政權，多半會對於人民的基本權力，如言論自由、集會結社等自由進行限制，以避免政權遭到挑戰，因此 (B) 較為適當，至於

　(A) 對政黨政治的競爭規則進行規範，只是民主開放程度的差異，但仍為民主國家；

　(C) 必要時宣布國家進入緊急狀態限制某些自由，縱為民主國家於國家面對危難時，仍會限制人民的自由；

　(D) 嚴格執行國家之法律，沒有商議妥協的餘地，此為國家法治程度的差異，不一定能判別民主化程度。

6. **A**

【解析】 (A) (B) (D) 依據『均權制度』的精神，地方政府在地方自治事項上擁有一定程度之『自治權』，因此地方議會有權在不抵觸中央法律的前提下，通過相關『自治條例』；

　(C) 該『自治條例』只要不抵觸法律即可，不須經立法院同意。

7. **D**

　【解析】　憲法本文第四條：『中華民國領土，依其固有之疆域，
　　　　　　非經國民大會之決議，不得變更之。』、憲法增修條文
　　　　　　第十一條：『自由地區與大陸地區間人民權利義務關係
　　　　　　及其他事務之處理，得以法律爲特別之規定。』，因此
　　　　　　憲法本文並未指明明確疆域範圍，而是在憲法增修條文
　　　　　　中依據兩岸現況明確使用『自由地區』與『大陸地區』
　　　　　　區別台灣與大陸，並無「中華臺北」、「中華民國臺灣
　　　　　　省」或「內地」等，政治權衡或通俗用語。

8. **B**

　【解析】　(A) 並無『每四年舉辦一次』之規定；
　　　　　　(B) 我國曾於 2008 年總統大選合併舉行「入聯」及
　　　　　　　　「返聯」公投；
　　　　　　(C) 公民投票並不能完全取代『公共政策的制定機制』，
　　　　　　　　而只是當政策具高度爭議性時，由人民親自抉擇，
　　　　　　　　因此並非公共政策制定最常用的方式；
　　　　　　(D) 我國並未針對 ECFA 案舉辦公民投票。

9. **A**

　【解析】　由圖一觀察，和平黨於 1991、1993 兩屆大選取得過半
　　　　　　席次，而正義黨則於 1996～2004 年四屆大選取得過半
　　　　　　席次，故該國係由和平及正義兩黨輪流執政，其他小
　　　　　　黨無法取得執政權，故爲『兩黨制』。

10. **A**

　【解析】　(A) 經濟問題源自於『慾望無窮，資源有限』，因此相
　　　　　　　　對於人類的慾望（希望常保年輕），青春仍是有限
　　　　　　　　的資源；

(B) 『稀少性』是相對於人類的慾望無窮而產生的『資源有限』問題，因此相對於人類的慾望，錢財仍具有稀少性的問題；

(C) 擔任志工對於社會的貢獻及正面的影響，遠高有形的報酬；

(D) 所謂的機會成本，是指選擇一種行為，必須放棄其他機會，而機會成本即是在所放棄的諸多選項中『價值最高的』，而依題意『遊覽各國』是當志工的附加價值，而非成本，因此『遊覽各國』並非當志工的機會成本，當志工的機會成本應該是，因為擔任志工而放棄的其他工作機會…等。

11. **C**

【解析】 (A) 瓶裝水並不會造成水資源的污染；

(B) (D) 瓶裝水的需求增加，會造成資源的浪費（如運費、包裝材料…等），但不至於造成水資源的耗竭。

12. **B**

【解析】 (A) (B) 店面、桌椅皆為人造的生產資源，屬於資本；

(C) 李媽媽為小吃店的經營者，因此其對於小吃口味的更新屬於企業能力，而非勞動；

(D) 李媽媽的兒子週末付出的時間屬於勞動的一部分。

13. **C**

【解析】 (A) 所謂共有財的悲歌，指某財物為大家所共有，所以每人在基於自己的最大利益考量下，便拚命使用導致資源耗竭，與題意無關

(B) 所謂資訊不完全，指交易的一方無法充分得知完整的資訊，最終使得市場僅剩劣質品供買方選購，亦與題意無關

(C) 依題意『當地政府雖與該工廠達成高額賠償金的共識，仍無法獲得當地居民的認同』，顯見當地居民認為爆炸所帶來的外部成本『大於』該工廠所認為的外部成本（廠商所願意付出的高額賠償金，即為外部成本內部化）

(D) 本題中並無『私有財產權界定不明確』的問題。

14. **B**

【解析】 依題意為「何種政策最有可能提高『我國』影片的國內票房占有率」，因此

(A) 調降隨電影票課徵之娛樂稅，將會降低票價（含國片、洋片），因此不一定『只會』提升『我國』影片的國內票房占有率

(B) 對外國影片之進口採配額限制，此舉將會限制外國影片進入國內市場，將有助於國片的發展

(C) 加強盜版影片的查緝，同樣包含國片及洋片，因此無助於提升『我國』影片的國內票房占有率

(D) 與外國簽署協定，增進雙方電影貿易，此舉有助於開拓國片的海外市場，但同時也必須開放更多國內市場給洋片。

15. **D**

【解析】 本題中抗議的議題雖是針對教育制度提出意見，但題目強調『抗議行為本身是在行使憲法所保障的何種基本權』，並非問其所關注的議題為何，因此在校園中遊行抗議並提出意見，為集會自由與言論自由的行使。

16. **A**

【解析】 依題意『員警盤查騎士，騎士不願接受盤查，大聲咆哮；員警先拉其下車，再以擒拿術壓制，限制行動…』，依上述情節員警可採錄影蒐證，逕行舉發等…對人民損害較小的方式取締，但員警卻採『擒拿術壓制，限制行動…』等強制手段，違反比例原則之必要性原則。

17. **C**

【解析】 (A) 警察機關訊問完畢後，應移送地檢署，經檢方偵辦後再決定是否向法院提起公訴。

(B) 『拘留』屬違反行政法上義務之處罰，是行政罰之一種，而本題所涉爲刑法，且若要先行『羈押』人犯，則須由法院依據刑事訴訟法第 101 條規定予以羈押，而非由警察機關主動羈押『被告經法官訊問後，認爲犯罪嫌疑重大，…非予羈押，顯難進行追訴、審判或執行者，得羈押之』。

(D) 依《犯罪被害人保護法》之規定『犯罪被害補償金之種類及支付對象如下：一、遺屬補償金：支付因犯罪行爲被害而死亡者之遺屬。二、重傷補償金：支付因犯罪行爲被害而受重傷者。三、性侵害補償金：支付因性侵害犯罪行爲而被害者。』，因此遭竊者無法要求政府補償。

18. **C**

【解析】 (A) 應改爲年滿二十歲；

(B) 未滿七歲才爲無行爲能力人；

(C) 滿七歲而未滿 20 歲的未成年人，若爲依其年齡和身分，日常生活所必需的行爲（如：購買考試用參考書），得不經法定代理人允許；

(D) 男性結婚年齡須滿十八，且仍須法定代理人同意。

19. **D**

　【解析】 (A) (D) 警察雖主張『取走 CD 光碟是爲維護社會秩序』，
　　　　　　　但在程序上仍應符合『正當法律程序』（進入店家
　　　　　　　並取走民衆財物（CD 光碟）是搜索、扣押的行爲，
　　　　　　　應取得法院核發的搜索票），才符合法治國原則的
　　　　　　　要求；

　　　　　 (B) 大聲播放歌曲表達支持，屬於言論自由的展現；

　　　　　 (C) 依刑事訴訟法第 128-1 條：『偵查中檢察官認有搜
　　　　　　　索之必要者，除第一百三十一條第二項所定情形
　　　　　　　外，應以書面記載前條第二項各款之事項，並敘述
　　　　　　　理由，聲請該管法院核發搜索票。』，依此搜索行
　　　　　　　爲若未經法院同意，而只是在檢察官的指揮下進
　　　　　　　行，『未必』就是合法的執行職務行爲。

20. **B**

　【解析】 法官於判決時，會依據刑法第 57 條之規定，衡量被告
　　　　　 犯罪時的一切情狀，給予適當合理的判決，因此判決時
　　　　　 一定會考慮被告（張生）所受的委屈，（刑法第 57 條
　　　　　 『科刑時應以行爲人之責任爲基礎，並審酌一切情狀，
　　　　　 尤應注意下列事項，爲科刑輕重之標準：一、犯罪之動
　　　　　 機、目的。二、犯罪時所受之刺激。三、犯罪之手段。
　　　　　 四、犯罪行爲人之生活狀況。五、犯罪行爲人之品行。
　　　　　 六、犯罪行爲人之智識程度。七、犯罪行爲人與被害人
　　　　　 之關係。八、犯罪行爲人違反義務之程度。九、犯罪所
　　　　　 生之危險或損害。十、犯罪後之態度。』）。

<u>21-22 為題組</u>

21. **D**

【解析】 所謂社會正義，依據羅爾斯的《正義論》主張，應具有
兩項特質：（一）保障每一個人的平等與自由；（二）
照顧社會中的弱勢階級的利益，因此『奢侈稅』的推
動，在於避免投資客『短進短出』炒作房地產，而使
一般民眾無力購屋，其目的在於保障人民基本生活及
居住需求。

22. **B**

【解析】 依題意『買方預期豪宅價格將下跌，導致市場需求減
少』，將使需求線左移，數量減少；『賣方因政策的
衝擊而不願將豪宅賣出，造成市場供給減少』，將使
供給線也左移，數量減少，但因題目並未說明兩者減
少幅度的多寡，因此只能確定數量一定減少，但價格
變化則無法判斷是否上漲、下跌或不變。

<u>23-24 為題組</u>

23. **C**

【解析】 (A) 認為「沒有經濟基礎」是其未結婚理由的比例，男
性明顯多於女性，因此 (A) 論點有可能；

(B) 除『經濟條件』外，該國男女尚會將『有無合適對
象』作為考慮項目，因此經濟條件並非唯一因素；

(C) 由圖二觀察，20-24 女性認為「沒有經濟基礎」為
其未結婚理由的比例為 23%，而 35-39 女性認為
「沒有經濟基礎」為其未結婚理由的比例則只有
6%，顯見「沒有經濟基礎」對未婚女性而言，年
紀愈輕結婚意願愈『容易』受到經濟壓力的影響；

(D) 針對「尚無合適對象」對未婚女性而言，在任何一個年齡層皆較男性高出許多，因此可推論就未婚男性而言，其結婚意願受到無合適對象的影響較女性來得小。

24. **A**

【解析】『平價社會住宅、生育補貼、公辦幼兒托育及減免國小學童學費等政策』皆可有助於減輕經濟負擔，而在圖二中因考量「沒有經濟基礎」而尚未結婚比例最高的族群為『30 至 34 歲的未婚男性』，因此該政策有助影響其結婚意願。

25. **B**

【解析】(B) 此題關鍵處在「鐵路電氣化」、「美援」這兩項，「鐵路電氣化」屬於十大建設之一，西部縱貫線全線 1979 年完工；「美援」從中華民國抗日作戰時已出現，1949 年國民政府播遷台灣後，停止援助直到韓戰爆發才繼續，從 1951 年到 1965 年，中華民國大約每年自華府得到大約一億美元的貸款，中華民國自從 1951 年到 1965 年總計接受美國經濟支援達 14.8 億美元；

(A) 1930 年代沒有研究「鐵路電氣化」的可能性；

(C) 1980 年代、(D) 1990 年代「鐵路電氣化」已完成、「美援」已結束，故不選。

26. **A**

【解析】(A) 春秋戰國最引人注目現象是貴族沒落，平民崛起，「君子陵夷，小人上升」；加上禮樂崩壞，春秋末期，鄭國子產「鑄刑書於鼎」（538B.C.），新成文

法時代來臨，由西周的封建特權時代走向「編戶齊
民」的社會，此舉引發鄰近晉國貴族之疑慮，認爲
人民可有成文法律做爲靠山，極可能威脅旣有的社
會穩定及政治秩序，證明平民興起漸成爲國家中堅
力量；

(B) 中國史上到明淸爲止君權不斷升高，民權未增強；

(C) 子產鑄刑書非鎮壓百姓，才有「引發鄰近晉國貴族
之疑慮，認爲人民可有成文法律做爲靠山，據此爭
取自身權益」；

(D) 中國帝王時代司法解釋和裁量向來屬於統治者，非
由人民主導。

27. **B**

【解析】 (B) 題目所講的「這個效忠儀式」就是歐洲中古時期封
建制度下領主與附庸的關係，歐洲中古從西元 476
年西羅馬帝國被蠻族滅掉，到十四世紀爲止，故
選 (B)；

(A) 八世紀前期君士坦丁堡屬於東羅馬帝國。

28. **D**

【解析】 (D) 1985 年蘇聯總統戈巴契夫對內採取民主和開放的改
革政策，對外採取和解政策，終止和美國的軍備競賽；
他的改革造成共產黨解散和蘇聯解體（組成「獨立國家
國協」），冷戰結束，華沙公約組織解體（1991 年），前
東歐共黨國家，如波蘭、捷克及匈牙利等華沙公約組
織原會員國改加入北大西洋公約組織。

29. **C**

　【解析】　(C) 此題關鍵處在「我們要關心現實，寫我們的現實」
　　　　　　點出是「1970 年代的鄉土文學」，中華民國在台灣文
　　　　　　學發展民國四十（1950）年代──反共文學、懷鄉文
　　　　　　學（成天做著新式或舊式的「鴛鴦蝴蝶夢」）、民國五
　　　　　　十（1960）年代－西方文化的衝擊（買辦、崇洋媚
　　　　　　外）、民國六十（1970）年代──鄉土化，不再迷戀西
　　　　　　方文化、民國七十（1980）年代──多元文化。

30. **C**

　【解析】　(C) 此題關鍵處在「十九世紀初，帝國甚至遭拿破崙解
　　　　　　散」，神聖羅馬帝國成立於 962 年鄂圖一世被羅馬
　　　　　　教皇加冕為羅馬的皇帝，到西元 1806 年遭拿破崙
　　　　　　解散；
　　　　　　(A) 俄羅斯帝國結束於 1917 年二月革命；
　　　　　　(B) 拜占庭帝國 1453 年被鄂圖曼土耳其帝國滅亡；
　　　　　　(D) 鄂圖曼帝國在一次世界大戰後解體。

31. **A**

　【解析】　(A) 十六世紀起因地理大發現的關係，西班牙成為歐洲
　　　　　　最富強的國家，西班牙國王菲利普為反制抗議教派，
　　　　　　避免其擴張，還願與教廷合作，免費將傳教士送往
　　　　　　商船所到之處傳教；
　　　　　　(B) 英格蘭、(D) 北歐瑞典屬於新教教區，國王不可能與
　　　　　　教廷合作；
　　　　　　(C) 俄國彼得大帝為十七到十八世紀俄羅斯帝國的皇
　　　　　　帝，不可能在十六世紀起出資組成船隊，前往印度
　　　　　　與東亞地區貿易，還與教廷合作，免費將傳教士送
　　　　　　往商船所到之處傳教。

32. **B**

【解析】 (B) 民國 8 年五四運動起因於巴黎和會山東問題偏袒日本，北京學生集會於天安門廣場抗議，影響民族意識高張、中國拒簽對德凡爾賽和約、把胡適之領導的新文化運動推向另一個高峰，故由論文裡的關鍵詞有「中日關係、山東問題、胡適、巴黎和會」可知為「五四運動」。

33. **C**

【解析】 (C) 三十年代經濟大恐慌（The Great Depression）起因美國孤立主義者主張提高關稅稅率，在關稅壁壘阻隔下，國際貿易幾陷停頓，1929 年紐約華爾街股票價格下瀉，許多人破產，公司、銀行、商店、工廠紛紛倒閉，形成全球經濟大恐慌,題幹敘述與「經濟大恐慌」最吻合。

34. **A**

【解析】 (A) 由題目中「臺灣原本不產耕牛，主政者負責引進牛隻繁殖」，可知是荷蘭時期；荷蘭人引進黃牛、蔬果等，如荷蘭豆（碗豆）、番薑（辣椒）、番介藍（包心菜）、蕃茄（柑仔蜜）、芒果、釋迦等入台灣，且出現第一波漢人移民潮,此即題目中『大量招募「中土遺民」前來開墾』。

35. **D**

【解析】 (D) 十八世紀啟蒙運動和十九世紀自由主義他們贊成「有限的民權」，即只有具有一定財產及教育水準的公民才有參政權，這種被稱為中產階級的意識形

態，題目中「國家應由受過良好教育、擁有財產的
人來管理」即爲此思想的表現；

(A) (B) 時期中產階級尙未出現，中產階級出現於 11-13
世紀十字軍東征後；

(C) 1215 年約翰簽署大憲章時中產階級勢力尙未發達。

36. **B**

【解析】(B) 北宋時期，政治中心依然在北方，故黃河中、下游
的市鎮數量很多；但同時期南方農工商業皆進步發
達，長江三角洲市鎮數量少，但每個市鎮的貿易額
都很大，北宋時，江南戶口數佔全國一半以上；

(A) 唐代前期政府不可能黃河中、下游和長江三角洲兩
個地區所收的商業稅大致相等；

(C) 蒙元時期，南北人口比例，高達八與二之比，華北
經濟漸趨沒落，不可能黃河中、下游和長江三角洲
收的商業稅大致相等；

(D) 明代時期，江南市鎮經濟擴大，明末有「湖廣熟，
天下足」之諺，不可能黃河中、下游和長江三角洲
收的商業稅大致相等。

37. **A**

【解析】(A) 由題幹「蕃人懾服」、「接受清國請求而撤軍，並將
該地人民交還清國」可知爲「牡丹社事件後日軍的
公告」，中的「蕃人」指排灣族人，和議指「北京
專約」；

(B) 日軍佔領琉球後未將該地人民交還清國；

(C) 甲午戰後日軍未將該地人民交還清國；

(D) 日俄戰爭日軍對象是俄國人。

38. **C**

【解析】 (C) 唐代發生銅幣面額低於其金屬價值的現象，故人民
　　　　將銅幣熔鑄成其他器物以牟利，為紓緩市場銅錢不足
　　　　問題，政府禁止民間鑄造銅器，除銅鏡之外，禁止民
　　　　間以銅為原料，鑄造器物；如唐德宗時，政府申明銅
　　　　一律由官方收購，規定除鑄造銅鏡以外，不得鑄造及
　　　　私相買賣（銅器）；在實行銅禁的同時，唐朝政府採取
　　　　多種辦法保證鑄幣材料供應，從而增加鑄幣量。

39. **D**

【解析】 (D) 清末在河南安陽出土的甲骨文書，主要內容多為占
　　　　卜的紀錄，亦稱「卜辭」、「貞卜文字」、「殷墟書契」，
　　　　不可能主要內容是土地交易契約，因為商代並無土地
　　　　交易行為，自然不可能有契約，應為贗品。

40. **C**

【解析】 (C) 元老院與公民大會出現在羅馬，羅馬共和末期陷於
　　　　軍閥對抗局面，最後由屋大維（Gaius Octavius）脫
　　　　穎而出，他了解人們緬懷共和的心理，保留元老院
　　　　與公民大會，並以「第一公民」（Princeps）自稱；
　　　　27B.C. 被元老院敬奉「奧古斯都」（Augustus）尊
　　　　號，集大權於一身，成為羅馬第一位皇帝，共和時
　　　　代結束；

　　　　(A) 亞歷山大大帝時無「元老院」；

　　　　(B) 凱撒是羅馬共和時期的將領，因獨裁被暗殺；

　　　　(D) 君士坦丁為羅馬帝國皇帝，非元老院選舉。

41. **D**

【解析】 (D) 神廟定期舉行「豐年慶典」足以證明農業定耕生活
　　　　　方式；

　　　　(A) 尼羅河定期氾濫國王須派人丈量土地，埃及人發展
　　　　　出進步的數學，尤其是三角學與幾何學、也使埃及
　　　　　人樂觀；

　　　　(B) 養育肥美魚類與畜牧業有關；

　　　　(C) 河岸有牲畜覓食與畜牧業有關。

42. **A**

【解析】 (A) 15 世紀中葉起莫斯科大公伊凡三世規定只有在 11
　　　　　月 26 日「尤里耶夫節」前後各一星期，農民才可
　　　　　以離開主人，農奴制度開始在全國範圍內確立；俄
　　　　　國於克里米亞戰爭（1854-56 年）失敗後，沙皇亞歷
　　　　　山大二世力圖改革，1861 年廢除農奴制，亞歷山大
　　　　　二世改革過程中受到相當大的阻力，亞歷山大二世
　　　　　後被暗殺身亡；一位俄國學者批評廢除農奴制，認
　　　　　為它「改變數百年習慣的生活方式，摧毀自古以來
　　　　　人民與土地的連結關係。」；

　　　　(B) 公社不是俄國十九世紀中期的政策；

　　　　(C) 十九世紀中期俄國未進行農地重劃；

　　　　(D) 土地國有為 1917 年十月革命後的政策。

43. **C**

【解析】 (C) 俄羅斯帝國，通常簡稱為俄國、帝俄或沙俄，是
　　　　　1721 年至 1917 年間俄羅斯國家的名稱；第一次
　　　　　世界大戰爆發，德軍分東西戰線，西線有兩列預
　　　　　計開赴比利時前線，另有一列即將駛往東方邊界
　　　　　－向沙俄宣戰；

(A) (B) 未分東西戰線；

(D) 1939 年歐洲大戰爆發，沙俄已於 1917 年結束。

44. **B**

【解析】 (B) 文藝復興時代的藝術家開始使用油畫原料，運用明暗對比法和透視法作畫，題幹中有「藝術創作強調恢復希臘與羅馬的傳統，藝術家精研人體結構，重視透視法」可知為十四世紀到十六世紀的文藝復興運動。

45. **C**

【解析】 (C) 台北八里大坌坑文化（粗繩紋陶文化），距今 7000－5000 年，分布在臺灣西半部及澎湖群島；生活以漁獵為主，已知原始農耕（燒墾、根莖類）；由題幹中「種植根莖類的作物」可知為「大坌坑文化」；

(A) (B) 屬於舊石器時代，當時尚未有農業；

(D) 金屬器時代。

46. **C**

【解析】 (C) 清代大租戶、小租戶的土地制度形成兩重地主和兩重佃農－大租戶（一級地主）、小租戶（二級地主兼一級佃農）及最下面的佃農，清代臺灣常發生小租戶人拖欠大租戶，以致於大租戶無力繳正供，影響到清代財政，故劉銘傳採用「減四留六」之法，在小租戶擁有法律上的土地所有權，但大租戶仍不能消滅；日治時期，總督府以將大租戶消除，以小租戶為新的地主階級，使得臺灣的土地制度步入了進代化，同時大租戶以政府發行的公債以及現金作為補償，無意的使土地財富間接的投資於資本主義之中。

47. **A**

【解析】(A) 此題講鴉片戰爭後中應簽訂南京條約及續約，使清朝喪失香港本島外，又損失領事裁判權、協定關稅、租界、片面最惠國待遇等四大主權，題幹「中國政府同意各國商品除繳交 5% 的進口關稅外，不用再繳納任何雜費」即指「協定關稅」。

48. **D**

【解析】(D) 題幹中「我們國內的科技、教育都比附近國家落後20 年」、「我們要靠普羅大眾。我相信我們一定會做得比日本好」可知是 1980 年代的中國，如鄧小平全力推動的「農業、工業、國防和科技」為重點的四個現代化；

(A) 1890 年代俄國國力不弱，甚至能插手歐陸事務，不可能「國內的科技、教育都比附近國家落後 20 年」；

(B) 1930 年代當世界經濟大恐慌時，德國希特勒政權藉由公共建設等方式復興經濟，重返強國地位；

(C) 印度於二次大戰後獨立，發展五年經濟計畫，帶動印度發展，不可能「國內的科技、教育都比附近國家落後 20 年」。

49. **B**

【解析】區位擴散：是企業考量各地工業區位的條件，選擇成本最低，產業獲得最高利潤的區位，使產業陸續擴散到各地的過程。文中之企業在台灣設廠、研發，陸續在江蘇、上海、荷蘭、四川設廠，可顯示企業有「區位擴張」現象。

(A) 一地區的許多工廠形成連鎖關係後，即使有其他更好的區位，工廠也不輕易遷離，形成「工業慣性」。

(C) 區位聚集：因工廠聚集使生產成本降低，產生聚集經濟。

(D) 空間移轉：指一地適合該產業發展的良好區位條件消失後，產業發生空間的轉移現象，產業可能完全轉移至新的區位生產製造。

50. **A**

【解析】 在無電腦製圖工具協助下，要繪製黑面琵鷺年中遷徙圖：

(1) 首先綜合國內、外觀察紀錄，找出黑面琵鷺遷徙路線的空間分布地點或經緯坐標的絕對位置，再將其繪於地圖上。

(2) 繪製地圖前須先「了解地圖的座標系統」，才能在地圖中標示出正確的遷徙路線之點位分布。

51. **A**

【解析】 附圖中顯示出四個時期的全球總貿易額的平均年增加率均大於總生產值的平均年增加率，可判讀出「全球分工盛行，使區域間相互依賴增強」，世界各國之間的貿易興旺，故全球總貿易額增加。

52. **B**

【解析】 1. 非洲的馬利、尼日、查德、塞內加爾和布吉納法索五國均在「撒赫爾」區，該區位於撒哈拉沙漠南側的半乾燥氣候區。

2. 撒赫爾區北部以 100 mm 等雨線爲界，南部以 600 mm 等雨線爲界，故北部是乾草原，爲游牧區，南部是莽原，實施半農半牧。根據當地氣候判斷最適宜的經濟作物應爲「棉花、花生」。

3. (A)(C)(D) 的作物多分布於溼潤的熱帶氣候區。

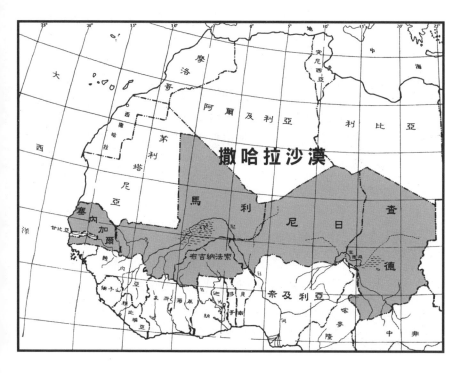

53. **D**

【解析】1. 此五國「以擴大經濟作物種植面積爲主要政策」、「以經濟作物的產品出口創造外匯，利用外匯進口糧食和工業製品的現象」判斷爲：以一級產業的廉價經濟作物爲出口導向的「殖民地式」的經濟型態。

2. (A) 物流：指物品運送流動的過程。

3. (B) 三角貿易：指歐洲（工業產品出口非洲）、非洲
   （黑奴輸往美洲）、美洲（農、礦資源出口歐洲）
   從 16 世紀起，三者之間的不對等貿易。

4. (C) 空間分工鏈：指製造區位的空間分工與連鎖，例
   如美、日高科技廠商選擇生產成本最低，且交通
   便利的地方，將技術轉移至中國和印度設廠。

54. **B**

【解析】 由表中可判讀出：中國原物料消耗占世界的比例甚高，
但 GDP 占世界的比例卻低，顯示中國以廉價的代工製
造為主，產品的附加價值不高，「作為世界工廠色彩
濃厚」。

55. **C**

【解析】 1. 中國與台灣均位於季風亞洲，冬季季風源於蒙古高
原的冷高壓地區，向海洋輻散，受科氏力的影響季
風偏向成為西北風、北風、東北風。

2. 冬季季風盛行季節，將中國沙塵暴的懸浮物與排放
的污染物隨風傳送到台灣，故「晚秋—冬季—初春
（11～3月）」對台影響最大。

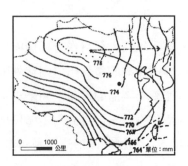

<u>56-58題爲題組</u>

56. **D**

【解析】 中國實施城鄉分隔制度，透過戶籍登記，形成都市居
　　　　民和農民，城市地區的社會保障、醫療保障只提供給
　　　　城市戶籍居民。在城市工作的農民工（盲流）無法設
　　　　戶籍，也無社會保障福利。

57. **C**

【解析】 表中的資料分爲六大地區的數量且加總比例爲 100%，
　　　　最適合用長條圖和圓餅圖表示資料的數量和比例。

　　　　甲、　曲線圖（折線圖）：以曲線之高低起伏表示時間
　　　　　　　或空間連續性的資料值變化情形。例如月均溫的
　　　　　　　曲線圖。

　　　　乙、　長條圖（柱狀圖）：以長柱的長短來表示數量或
　　　　　　　百分比之大小。例如月雨量的柱狀圖、2010 年全
　　　　　　　球六大地區國外旅客到訪人數的長條圖。

　　　　丙、　圓餅圖：使用在資料類別少，依據各組成要素占
　　　　　　　總量的 %，以圓的扇形瓣來表示，資料加總比
　　　　　　　例爲 100%。例如：台灣區 100 年度稅收來源圓
　　　　　　　餅圖、2010 年全球六大地區觀光外匯收入的圓
　　　　　　　餅圖。

　　　　丁、　等值線圖：將數值相同各點，用平滑曲線相連繪
　　　　　　　製而成，能顯示數值的空間變化且連續分布的自
　　　　　　　然現象。例如等高線圖、等溫線圖。

58. **D**

【解析】 1. 表中資料顯示出歐洲地區的國外旅客到訪人數占全球 50.7%，觀光外匯收入占全球 44.7%，觀光遊憩業最發達。

2. 歐洲位中高緯度的大陸西岸，沿海深受西風帶和北大西洋暖流的影響，以溫帶海洋性氣候與溫帶地中海型氣候為主。

59-60題為題組

59. **C**

【解析】 以「遊憩資源的遊客來源範圍」來定義商圈大小，則丙國家風景區總遊客數最多，故可判斷商圈最大。

60. **A**

【解析】 1. 台灣離島地區因冬季東北季風強勁，風強浪大，故冬季的氣候較不適宜觀光，夏季為觀光旺季。

2. 表中甲、乙兩區的遊客冬季偏低，夏季則遊客大增，可判斷最可能位於離島。（甲：澎湖國家風景區、乙：馬祖國家風景區）。

61-62題為題組

61. **B**

【解析】 1. 地質古老及火山分布地區，多金屬礦蘊藏。

2. 文中「有些地區地質古老」：指南美東部的巴西高原為古老結晶岩地塊，故多金屬礦。

3. 題目中「有些地區火山活動頻繁」：指中、南美洲西側位於太平洋「火環帶」，地殼不穩定，多火山、地震，因火山作用多金屬礦。

62. **A**

　　【解析】　1. 溫帶地中海型氣候的特有作物：葡萄、柑橘、橄欖、無花果等。

　　　　　　　2. 地中海型氣候分布在中緯度 30°～40° 的大陸西岸，
　　　　　　　　　(A) 智利：位南美洲大陸的西岸，故中部屬地中海型氣候。（北部為熱帶沙漠，南部為溫帶海洋性氣候）。

　　　　　　　3. (B) 烏拉圭：位南美洲大陸東岸。(C) 墨西哥：位中美洲高原。(D) 玻利維亞：位南美洲高地。

63-64題為題組

63. **B**

　　【解析】　1. 首要型都市：除了一個特大型的都市外，其餘均為中、小型都市。通常出現在區域經濟發展不均、都市化歷史短暫，或歷史上曾為殖民地的地區。

　　　　　　　2. 中南美洲首要型都市與殖民背景有關，沿海港埠型都市快速興起，內陸發展落後，區域經濟發展不均，貧富差距大，鄉村人口湧入都市謀生。

64. **C**

　　【解析】　1. 網格式資料（網格模式）：地理資訊以矩陣或方形網格為基本單元，將整個區域劃分為規則的網格，遙測衛星影像是典型的例子。

　　　　　　　2. 向量式資料（向量模式）：將地理現象化為點、線、面等元素，用（x, y）連續座標組的方式儲存。
　　　　　　　　　(A) (B) (D) 選項是由向量模式的線資料繪成，可表達地表現象的長度資訊。例如道路、河流、管線、等高線圖，或抽象的經緯線、行政界線圖等。

65-67 為題組

65. **C**

【解析】 根據附圖之經緯度座標（120°40′17″E，22°32′17″N）及圖中顯現的地形，判斷出位於台灣西南部的山麓平原區，適宜規畫發展熱帶栽培業。

66. **C**

【解析】 由衛星影像圖可判讀地形：地圖的上方為山地丘陵，下方為山麓平原，河流主要流向為西北向東南流，最符合此圖的數值立體地形圖為「丙圖」。

67. **A**

【解析】 1. 依據聯合國發布的「人類發展程度指標（HDI）」，可將全球分為極高度發展、高度發展、中度發展、低度發展國家。

2. 甲、乙兩國：數值低於 0.5 則屬低度發展國，其都市化程度也低。

68-70 為題組

68. **D**

【解析】 低穩定階段的人口特色：出生率低、死亡率低，老年人口比例高。丙、丁兩國老年人口比例最高，最可能進入「低穩定階段」。

69. **D**

【解析】 1. 「HDI」是①預期壽命②教育程度③人均 GDP，三指數的平均數。

　　2. 丙國平均壽命與國民平均就學年數都比丁國高，但
　　　　丙、丁的 HDI 數值相同，故可推估丁國的平均每人
　　　　國民生產毛額 GDP 高於丙國。

　　3. 甲國的平均壽命與國民平均就學年數比乙國高，但
　　　　甲、乙兩國的 HDI 數值相同，故推估乙國的人均
　　　　GDP 高於甲國。因此平均每人國民生產毛額排序
　　　　爲：丁丙甲乙。

70. **C**

【解析】　1. 省道台 9 線：爲南北向公路，由路標所顯示的城市
　　　　　　（鳳林、壽豐、花蓮）可判斷位中央山脈與海岸山
　　　　　　脈之間。

　　　　　2. (A) 台 1 線：台灣西部幹道。(B) 台 3 線：西部丘陵
　　　　　　山地區省道。(D) 台 61 線：西濱快速公路。

<u>71-72 爲題組</u>

71. **C**

【解析】　台灣台中盆地、彰化平原、濁水溪流域（彰、雲、投）
　　　　　一帶爲最重要的蔬菜和花卉等農產品的供應地，丙圖
　　　　　經台中市霧峰、南投縣草屯、南投市，故台 3 線最可
　　　　　能。

72. **A**

【解析】　路標座落地點，依南北向相對位置判斷：（低緯→高
　　　　　緯排列）甲（高雄市）→乙（花蓮縣）→丙（彰化縣）
　　　　　→丁（桃園縣）。

101 年大學入學學科能力測驗試題
自然考科

第壹部分（佔 96 分）

一、單選題（佔 56 分）

說明：第 1 題至第 28 題，每題均計分。每題有 n 個選項，其中只有
一個是正確或最適當的選項，請畫記在答案卡之「選擇題答案
區」。每題答對者，得 2 分；答錯、未作答或畫記多於一個選
項者，該題以零分計算。

1. 人類胚胎發育時，細胞迅速進行分裂與生長，並生成細胞膜，細
胞膜的成分<u>不含</u>下列哪一種成分？
   (A) 蛋白質 　　　　　　(B) 脂質 　　　　　　(C) 醣類
   (D) 去氧核糖核酸 　　　(E) 膽固醇

2. 圖1為植物細胞處於「有絲分裂後期」之示意圖。甲至戊五種構
造，哪一個不應出現於圖中？
   (A) 甲 　　　(B) 乙 　　　(C) 丙
   (D) 丁 　　　(E) 戊

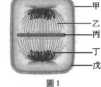

圖1

<u>3～4題為題組</u>

　　科學家針對五種不同品種的水稻（甲、乙、丙、丁及戊）進行基
因多樣性之研究，在各品種的個體間隨機取樣，檢測六個基因的基因
型種類。結果顯示各品種的每個基因平均都有十種不同的基因型。種
植十代後，再於各品種的個體間隨機取樣，檢測同樣六個基因的基因
型種類，得出平均每一個基因所具有的基因型種類數如表一所示：

表一

品種	親代數量（株）	親代基因型（種類）	子代（F10）數量（株）	子代（F10）基因型（種類）
甲	100	10	3000	10
乙	50	10	200	20
丙	100	10	2000	40
丁	60	10	1200	30
戊	200	10	6000	15

　　如果目前出現一種新的病毒會感染水稻，引起疾病，回答3～4題。

3. 新病毒引發水稻疾病後，上述哪一品種的水稻，因該種疾病而滅
　　絕的可能性最大？
　　(A) 甲　　　　(B) 乙　　　　(C) 丙　　　　(D) 丁　　　　(E) 戊

4. 下列有關會引發該水稻疾病之病原體的敘述，何者正確？
　　(A) 該病原體不能在寄主細胞內合成蛋白質
　　(B) 該病原體可進行有性生殖
　　(C) 該病原體一定具有DNA
　　(D) 該病原體兼具DNA及RNA
　　(E) 該病原體單獨存在時，不具有生命現象

5～6題為題組

　　圖2為一個虛擬的食物網，「甲」～「辛」
分別代表構成此食物網的八種物種，箭頭方向
表示兩者間有食性關係，例如圖中己→庚，表
示己為獵物，庚為掠食者。
根據圖2回答5～6題：

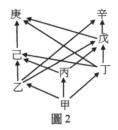
圖 2

5. 圖2虛擬的食物網中，下列哪一選項中之各物種間的競爭較激烈？
   (A) 乙丙丁
   (B) 丙戊庚
   (C) 甲庚辛
   (D) 丁戊辛
   (E) 甲乙己

6. 假設某種獵物有多個掠食者，且各掠食者對該獵物所造成的死亡率相同（至少5%）。若食物網中的物種「戊」全部滅絕，則下列哪一物種會最直接的受到影響而出現族群快速增長的情形？
   (A) 甲   (B) 乙   (C) 丙   (D) 丁   (E) 己

7. 圖3中的橫軸為年平均降雨量，縱軸為年平均溫度；甲～戊代表五種不同的陸域生態系的分布範圍，則何者最可能為針葉林？
   (A) 甲
   (B) 乙
   (C) 丙
   (D) 丁
   (E) 戊

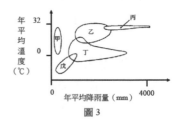

圖 3

8. 某水產試驗所想要復育X魚種與Y魚種。該試驗所已知X魚種與Y魚種在不同溫度與鹽度的環境下，個別族群增長量的結果如圖4。目前試驗所擁有甲～丁四種不同飼養條件的養殖池，如表二所示。

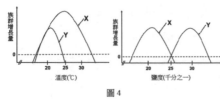

圖 4

表二

養殖池代號	溫度（℃）	鹽度（千分之一）
甲	20～25	28～33
乙	25～30	28～33
丙	20～25	18～23
丁	25～30	18～23

下列有關魚種與養殖池的配對，何者最適合？

	X魚種養殖池	Y魚種養殖池
(A)	丁	乙
(B)	丙	甲、丁
(C)	甲、丙	乙
(D)	丙、丁	甲
(E)	甲、乙	丙、丁

9. 在觀測條件良好的情況下，當我們仰望星空，在仙女座中可以看
   到一個稱為M31的渦狀星系，在獵戶座可以看到一個稱為M42的
   發射星雲，而M42的影像比M31小。下列有關此兩天體與太陽的
   距離之敘述，何者正確？
   (A) 因為M天體編號以距離遠近排序，所以M42的距離比M31遠
   (B) M42距離比M31遠，所以看起來比較小
   (C) 雖然M31是星系而M42是星雲，但兩者距離差不多
   (D) 因為M31是星系，所以M31距離遠比M42遠
   (E) 因為M42位於獵戶座，M42的距離比M31遠

10. 當我們在晴朗的夜晚仰望天空，看見滿天繁星，其中幾乎都是恆
    星，只有少數幾顆是行星。古今對恆星與行星的定義不同，古人
    如何判斷哪些光點是行星？
    (A) 由顏色判斷，恆星的顏色與行星不同
    (B) 恆星本身發光，而行星本身不發光
    (C) 恆星本身發光，而行星是反射陽光
    (D) 由它們在天上移動的軌跡來判斷
    (E) 恆星都比較暗，行星都比恆星亮

11. 板塊構造學說中有三種板塊邊界，隱沒帶為其中一種板塊邊界的構造，有關隱沒帶的特性，下列敘述何者正確？
    (A) 隱沒帶附近的海洋地殼較中洋脊附近的年輕
    (B) 隱沒帶為地殼密度最均勻的地方
    (C) 隱沒帶是張裂性板塊邊界
    (D) 岩石圈被帶至隱沒帶深處
    (E) 於隱沒帶產生的地震波僅傳遞至地心方向

12. 山崩是臺灣常見的天然災害。下列有關山崩的敘述，何者正確？
    (A) 山崩即為因重力作用而落下岩石或土壤的現象
    (B) 僅有順向坡的山區會發生山崩
    (C) 僅有變質岩為主的山區會發生山崩
    (D) 岩石經風化作用後就會發生山崩
    (E) 可藉由工程的手段完全阻止山崩的發生

13. 在北半球海洋，有一順時鐘方向旋轉且直徑超過100公里的大型旋渦，僅考慮其受科氏力的作用影響之下，此旋渦哪一區域的表面水位最高？
    (A) 東、西兩側　　　(B) 外圍　　　(C) 南側
    (D) 北側　　　(E) 中央

14. 在密度差異大到明顯分成上、下兩層的穩定海域，最可能出現下列哪一種現象？
    (A) 上層海水營養鹽較多　　(B) 上、下層海水混合作用強
    (C) 上層海水的CO_2較高　　(D) 下層海水溶氧較少
    (E) 下層海水溫度較高

15. 冬季時假設北京和高雄的地面氣壓相同，但是北京的地面溫度遠
　　比高雄的地面溫度低，則下列哪一敘述<u>不正確</u>？

　　(A) 北京的飽和水氣壓比高雄的飽和水氣壓低

　　(B) 北京的近地面空氣密度比高雄的近地面空氣密度大

　　(C) 北京與高雄兩地單位面積上空的空氣重量大約相同

　　(D) 北京的地面露點溫度一般比高雄的地面露點溫度低

　　(E) 近地面處北京的氣壓隨高度下降的變化比高雄慢

16. 根據氣象學家推估，2010年及2011年的一些異常天氣或氣候現象，
　　似乎和這兩年的反聖嬰現象有所關聯。下列有關「反聖嬰」現象
　　的敘述，何者正確？

　　(A) 赤道向西吹之貿易風（信風）減弱

　　(B) 南美洲西岸沿海的湧升流減弱

　　(C) 溫暖的海水向東移到東太平洋

　　(D) 澳洲達爾文港的氣壓比大溪地的氣壓高

　　(E) 東南亞與澳洲北部等鄰近地區的大氣對流活動增強

17. 王老師上高一基礎化學第一章緒論，介紹了化學簡史，並且強調
　　先進化學技術對生活的影響。學生上課後討論心得，下列哪些說
　　法合理？

　　(甲)實驗是物質科學的基礎，也是學習化學的有效途徑

　　(乙)道耳頓創立「原子學說」，奠定了化學的重要基礎

　　(丙)化學技術已可以研製一些原來自然界不存在的新材料

　　(丁)天然有機食物不是化合物，是最符合健康的食物

　　(戊)石化工業使用的輕油裂解技術，提供了取代化石燃料的新能源

　　(A) 甲乙　　　　　　(B) 丙丁　　　　　　(C) 丁戊

　　(D) 甲乙丙　　　　　(E) 乙丁戊

18. 已知一定質量的無水乙醇（C_2H_5OH）完全燃燒時，放出的熱量爲 Q，而其所產生的CO_2用過量的澄清石灰水完全吸收，可得0.10莫耳的$CaCO_3$沉澱。若1.0莫耳無水乙醇完全燃燒時，放出的熱量最接近下列哪一選項？

(A) Q   (B) 5Q   (C) 10Q   (D) 20Q   (E) 50Q

19. 對某一濃度爲0.01 M的未知水溶液進行測試，觀察到下列現象：

(1) 此溶液具有極佳導電性

(2) 此溶液的pH值和純水相近

(3) 此溶液通入二氧化碳，會產生白色沉澱

(4) 此溶液加入等體積的0.01 M氫氧化鈉溶液，會產生白色沉澱

此水溶液最可能含有下列何種物質？

(A) 氯化鈉   (B) 氯化鈣   (C) 蔗糖

(D) 碳酸鈉   (E) 氫氧化鉀

20. 圖5及圖6分別代表$H_2O_{(g)}$和$NO_{(g)}$的生成反應過程中，反應物與生成物的能量變化，則下列敘述何者正確？

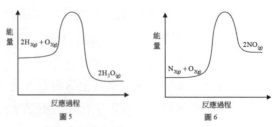

圖 5   圖 6

(A) $H_2O_{(g)}$的生成反應爲吸熱反應

(B) $NO_{(g)}$的生成反應爲吸熱反應

(C) $H_{2(g)}$燃燒產生水蒸氣的反應爲吸熱反應

(D) $NO_{(g)}$分解爲氮氣和氧氣的反應爲吸熱反應

(E) $H_2O_{(g)}$分解爲氫氣與氧氣的反應爲放熱反應

21. 三個靜止的物體甲、乙、丙，同時開始在水平面上作直線運動，
　　其運動分別以下列三圖描述：圖7為甲的位移與時間的關係，圖8
　　為乙的速度與時間的關係，圖9為丙的加速度與時間的關係。在
　　時間為5秒時，甲、乙、丙三者的加速度量值關係為何？

(A) 甲＝乙＜丙　　　　(B) 甲＝丙＜乙　　　　(C) 甲＜乙＝丙

(D) 甲＞乙＞丙　　　　(E) 丙＜甲＜乙

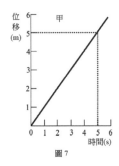
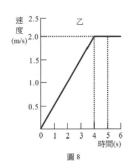
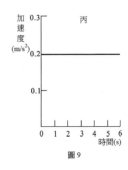

圖7　　　　　　　　　　圖8　　　　　　　　　　圖9

22. 高空彈跳者一躍而下，繩索伸長到最大長度時將彈跳者往上拉回，
　　接著彈跳者又落下，然後再被繩索拉回，接連重複數次。在這彈跳
　　過程中，下列何種能量轉換最不可能發生？

(A) 彈性位能轉換為重力位能　　　　(B) 彈性位能轉換為動能

(C) 重力位能轉換為動能　　　　　　(D) 動能轉換為重力位能

(E) 阻力產生的熱能轉換為動能

23. 氦原子核的電荷是質子電荷的2倍，而其質量則是質子質量的4
　　倍。假設一質子和一氦原子核，彼此只受到來自對方的靜電力作
　　用，則當質子所受靜電力的量值為 F 時，氦原子核所受靜電力的
　　量值為何？

(A) $\dfrac{1}{4}F$　　(B) $\dfrac{1}{2}F$　　(C) F　　(D) $2F$　　(E) $4F$

24. 岸上教練對潛入水中的學生大聲下達指令，在聲波由空氣傳入水中的過程中，下列有關聲波性質的敘述，何者正確？
    (A) 聲波的強度在水中較空氣中強
    (B) 聲波的頻率在水中與空氣中相同
    (C) 聲波的速率在水中較空氣中小
    (D) 聲波的波長在水中與空氣中相同
    (E) 聲波前進的方向在水中與空氣中相同

25. 在太空中，太空人在太空船外工作時，身穿太空衣以防熱能散失至太空中，主要是要防止太空人何種方式的熱傳播？
    (A) 傳導　　　　　　(B) 輻射　　　　　　(C) 對流
    (D) 熱質流動　　　　(E) 傳導與對流

26. 圖10中甲、乙、丙為大小相同且位置固定的三個同軸圓線圈，三圈面相互平行且與連接三圓心的軸線垂直。當三線圈通有同方向、大小均為I的穩定電流時，若僅考慮電流 I 所產生的磁場，下列有關此三線圈所受磁力方向的敘述，何者正確？
    (A) 甲線圈受到乙線圈的吸引力，丙線圈則受到乙線圈的排斥力
    (B) 甲線圈受到乙線圈的排斥力，丙線圈則受到乙線圈的吸引力
    (C) 甲、丙兩線圈均受到乙線圈的排斥力
    (D) 甲、丙兩線圈均受到乙線圈的吸引力
    (E) 三線圈間無磁力相互作用

甲乙丙
圖 10

27-28為題組

　　圖11為電力輸送系統的示意圖。發電廠為了將產生的電力輸送到用戶，先利用變壓器將交流電壓升到很高，經過高壓電塔間的兩條傳輸線甲及乙，輸送到遠地方的變電所再將電壓降低，然後分配給各個工廠與家庭。調整變壓器中的線圈數，可以改變電壓的升降比值。

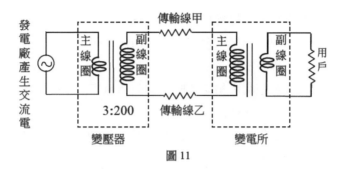

圖 11

27. 若發電廠產生的交流電壓為6,000伏特,變壓器主、副線圈的圈數比為3:200,則在發電廠變壓器副線圈的輸出電壓為多少伏特?
(A) 4×10^6
(B) 4×10^5
(C) 2×10^4
(D) 2×10^3
(E) 90

28. 若傳輸線輸送的電功率保持不變,而發電廠變壓器主、副線圈的圈數比,由原來的3:200改為3:100,則傳輸線因熱效應而消耗的電功率,變為原來的多少倍?
(A) 4
(B) 2
(C) $\dfrac{1}{2}$
(D) $\dfrac{1}{4}$
(E) 不變

二、多選題(佔 30 分)

說明:第 29 題至第 43 題,每題均計分。每題有 n 個選項,其中至少有一個是正確的選項,請將正確選項畫記在答案卡之「選擇題答案區」。各題之選項獨立判定,所有選項均答對者,得 2 分;答錯 k 個選項者,得該題 n-2k/n 的分數;但得分低於零分或所有選項均未作答者,該題以零分計算。

29. 一般複式顯微鏡常用於觀察生物切片,下列有關顯微鏡的構造與使用的敘述,哪些正確?(應選2項)

(A) 接目鏡與接物鏡均為凸透鏡

(B) 光源經由接物鏡後穿透生物切片，其影像再經由接目鏡加以放大觀察

(C) 進行觀察生物切片時，應先使用高倍率的接物鏡以利快速的找到欲觀察的構造

(D) 當接物鏡由4倍換成40倍時，視野中所涵蓋的樣本面積為原來的100倍

(E) 以5倍接目鏡配合40倍接物鏡，與以10倍接目鏡配合20倍接物鏡，兩者放大倍率相同

30. 小美到超市買了海帶、玉米、鳥巢蕨、香菇、酵母菌、番茄、四季豆及石花菜。就目前習得的生物五界系統分類而言，下列有關這些食物分類的敘述，哪些正確？（應選2項）

(A) 這些食物歸屬於四個界　　　(B) 香菇與海帶屬於同一界

(C) 酵母菌與石花菜屬於同一界　(D) 鳥巢蕨與玉米屬於同一界

(E) 番茄與四季豆屬於同一界

31. 沿岸海域有上升流（湧升流）現象的地方，與相鄰且沒有上升流的其他海域相比，其主要特色包括下列哪幾項？（應選3項）

(A) 白天海上吹向陸地的海風較強

(B) 海面較易形成霧　　　　(C) 表層海水密度較低

(D) 表層海水溫度下降　　　(E) 表層海水溶氧量增加

32. 地球形成的過程中曾經有一段時期處於熔融的狀態，之後逐漸冷卻下來演變成初始地球。下列哪些選項的事件是在約四十億年前，地球由形成初始時期的熔融狀態逐漸冷卻而產生的結果？

（應選3項）

(A) 海洋的形成　　　　　　　(B) 三葉蟲的出現

(C) 大氣層的形成　　　　　　(D) 大氣層中大量氧氣的形成

(E) 地球內部地核、地函及地殼的分層

33. 大尺度的天氣系統影響不大時，海、陸風是臺灣常見的局部環流
現象。下列有關臺灣海、陸風環流的敘述，哪些選項是正確的？
（應選2項）

(A) 陸風通常比海風強

(B) 陸風通常在傍晚時達到最強

(C) 海風吹到的地方，一般相對濕度會增加

(D) 最強的海風大約發生在午後時段

(E) 海風的風向並不是從高壓吹向低壓，而是大約平行於等壓線

34. 下列哪些物質是由共價鍵所形成的？（應選2項）

(A) 三氧化二鐵　　　　　　　(B) 青銅

(C) 四氧化二氮　　　　　　　(D) 氯化氫

(E) 十八開金（K金）

35. 家庭廚房中常用的調味品有食鹽、米酒與食醋。其中，食鹽的主要
成分是氯化鈉，米酒中含有乙醇，食醋中則含有乙酸。下列有關
此三種物質的敘述，哪些正確？（應選2項）

(A) 此三種物質的水溶液，食鹽與米酒呈中性，食醋呈酸性

(B) 此三種物質的水溶液，在相同濃度時，以食醋的導電性最好

(C) 氯化鈉、乙醇與乙酸中，以氯化鈉的熔點最低

(D) 乙醇與乙酸屬於分子化合物

(E) 氯化鈉易溶於揮發性有機溶劑

36. 日常飲食中，會接觸到各類的化學物質。下列敘述哪些正確？
（應選2項）

   (A) 綠茶與咖啡中的咖啡因，對多數人具有提神效果

   (B) 纖維素為醣類，可被人體消化，分解成葡萄糖

   (C) 蛋白質是由胺基酸聚合而成，是人體生長所需要的物質

   (D) 食品中添加寡醣，是因其分子較葡萄糖小，容易被人體吸收

   (E) 澱粉與蔗糖皆屬聚合物，是由很多小分子結合而成的巨大分子

37. 下列哪些化學反應是由「單一元素的物質與化合物反應，產生另
   一種單一元素的物質和他種化合物」？（應選2項）

   (A) 氫氣還原氧化銅　　　　(B) 一氧化碳在氧中燃燒

   (C) 一氧化碳還原氧化銅　　(D) 銀棒放入硫酸銅溶液

   (E) 鋅棒放入硫酸銅溶液

38. 某離子交換樹脂的裝置如圖12所示：甲管裝填RNa型陽離子交換
   樹脂，乙管裝填R'OH型陰離子交換樹脂。當含硫酸鈣的水溶液依
   序通過甲、乙兩管時，下列哪些敘述正確？（應選2項）

   (A) 在甲管內，鈣離子會與氫離子交換

   (B) 當甲管的交換率降低後，可用飽和食鹽水再生

   (C) 在乙管內，硫酸根離子會與氫離子交換

   (D) 在乙管內，硫酸根離子會與氫氧根離子
      交換

   (E) 當乙管交換率降低後，可用鹽酸再生

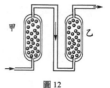

圖12

39. 張同學用U型管進行「電解碘化鉀溶液」的實驗時，以白金作正
   極（陽極）、黃金作負極（陰極），電解0.1 M碘化鉀水溶液。
   下列有關此電解實驗的敘述，哪些正確？（應選2項）

(A) 陰極附近的溶液會變成酸性

(B) 陽極附近的溶液出現黃褐色

(C) 在陰極附近，會有氣泡冒出，這些氣泡是氧氣

(D) 取陰極附近的溶液約2毫升於試管，然後加入酚酞指示劑數滴並振盪試管，則呈現粉紅色

(E) 取陽極附近的溶液約2毫升於試管，然後加入1毫升的正己烷。振盪試管後靜置5分鐘，成為混濁的乳液

40. 下列各組物質中，哪些互為同分異構物？（應選2項）

(A) 氧與臭氧　　　(B) 葡萄糖與果糖　　(C) 金剛石與碳六十

(D) 蛋白質與耐綸　(E) 蔗糖與麥芽糖

41. 下列關於液晶彩色電視及電漿彩色電視比較的敘述，哪些是錯誤的？（應選2項）

(A) 兩者皆可接收來自空中電磁波的影像訊號

(B) 兩者顯像過程皆需要外加電壓以建立電場

(C) 兩者皆可顯示各種不同的色彩

(D) 兩者皆是利用不同電場改變物質分子排列，造成各像素明暗差異

(E) 兩者皆是利用電子撞擊螢光幕上紅、藍、綠三色的小點構成像素，來顯現色彩

42. 下列的光源及光學元件組合可以用來進行光學實驗，哪些較適合觀察光的色散現象？（應選2項）

(A) 單色光雷射及一個凸透鏡　　(B) 太陽及一個三稜鏡

(C) 綠光雷射筆及一個凹透鏡

(D) 白熾電燈及一顆透明的玻璃彈珠

(E) 紅色發光二極體（LED）燈及一塊透明的玻璃

43. 夜間潛水時，水面下的人與岸上的另一人以光互傳訊息，如圖13
所示，圖中乙與戊為光不偏折的路徑。下列哪些選項為光訊息可
能的行進路徑？（應選2項）

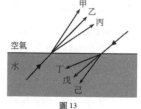

圖 13

(A) 甲
(B) 乙
(C) 丙
(D) 丁
(E) 己

三、綜合題（佔 10 分）

說明：第 44 題至第 48 題，共 5 題，每題均計分，每題有 n 個選項，
其中只有一個是正確或最適當的選項，請畫記在答案卡之「選
擇題答案區」。各題答對者，得 2 分；答錯、未作答或畫記多
於一個選項者，該題以零分計算。

<u>請閱讀下列短文後，回答第44-48題</u>

　　科學的創新研究不但開創新的研究領域，也促使科技進步，而新
科技又常導致科學上的新發現。例如居禮夫婦與貝克勒發現某些物質
具放射性，導致居禮夫人又發現釙（Po）和鐳（Ra）兩個具放射性的
元素。不但在科學上開創新領域，時至今日放射性元素更有廣泛的應
用。X光的發現是另外一個例子。X光是侖琴在1895年進行陰極射線管
實驗時意外發現的，後來成為醫學、科學與工業上重要的檢測工具，
特定波長檢測用的X光為原子受激發至高能態後躍遷至低能態而發出
的電磁波。華生與克里克兩人在1953年提出了DNA構造的雙股螺旋模
型，開啟了分子生物學及遺傳學的新篇章，這項劃時代的發現，多少
歸功於X光對DNA結構的剖析；天文學家在20世紀發現太陽、恆星與
星系都會發出X光，成為研究宇宙與星體演化的工具。

44. 圖14為利用X光觀察DNA所繪出之立體的雙股結構示意圖；圖中的 θ 代表DNA結構旋轉的角度，其中Y段雙股的DNA共含有多少個含氮鹼基？

(A) 8

(B) 10

(C) 12

(D) 16

(E) 20

(F) 24

圖14

45. DNA雙股配對原則為A與T配對，C與G配對。假如一段DNA5'-ATCGC-3'與其互補股間共有13個氫鍵，則某段DNA其中一股的序列為5'-AACGGTCGCATCGGTCATGC-3'，則該段DNA兩股間應有多少個氫鍵？

(A) 20　　(B) 40　　(C) 48　　(D) 52　　(E) 60

46. 天文學家常用X光望遠鏡觀測星系碰撞現象，下列地點中何者最適合架設X光望遠鏡？

(A) 視野遼闊的高原，如西藏高原

(B) 沒有光害的高山，如夏威夷的毛拉基亞山

(C) 大氣擾動少的沙漠，如美國新墨西哥州

(D) 環繞地球的軌道上，但在范艾倫輻射帶中

(E) 環繞地球的軌道上，但在范艾倫輻射帶外

47. 下列關於$_{84}$Po（質量數210）原子及$_{88}$Ra（質量數226）原子的敘述，何者正確？

(A) $_{84}^{210}$Po和$_{88}^{226}$Ra兩種原子核中的中子數相差16

(B) $_{84}^{210}$Po和$_{88}^{226}$Ra兩種原子核中的質子數相差16

(C) $_{84}^{210}$Po和$_{88}^{226}$Ra兩種原子中的電子數相差4

(D) 釙和鐳兩個元素,在自然界都不存在

(E) 釙和鐳的放射性都是源自其原子核釋出X光

48. 醫學診斷常利用超音波(超聲波)、內視鏡或特定波長的X光來進行檢查。一旦發現病因,也可能使用放射線等來進行治療。這些現代科技可能涉及下列的物理原理:

(甲)原子核衰變　　　　　　　　(乙)波的反射和透射

(丙)原子由高能態躍遷至低能態而輻射

(丁)波以夠大的入射角射向折射率較低的介質時,會完全反射

下表中所列的技術與原理之對應,何者是最恰當的?

科技選項	超音波(超聲波)	內視鏡	放射線	特定波長的X光
(A)	乙	丙	甲	丁
(B)	甲	丁	丙	乙
(C)	乙	丁	甲	丙
(D)	丁	甲	乙	丙
(E)	丙	乙	丁	甲

第貳部分 (佔32分)

說明: 第49題至第68題,每題2分。單選題答錯、未作答或畫記多於一個選項者,該題以零分計算;多選題每題有 n 個選項,答錯 k 個選項者,得該題 n-2k/n 的分數;但得分低於零分或所有選項均未作答者,該題以零分計算。此部分得分超過32分以上,以滿分32分計。

49. 圖15為植物細胞在放入各種溶液前，以及放入甲、乙及丙三種不同濃度的蔗糖溶液後，細胞變化情形的示意圖。下列哪些敘述正確？（應選2項）

(A) 植物細胞在甲溶液中膨壓最大

(B) 植物細胞在乙溶液中無水分子進出

實驗處理	置放前	甲溶液	乙溶液	丙溶液
細胞變化情形				

圖 15

(C) 丙溶液的蔗糖濃度最低

(D) 放入甲溶液後，植物細胞內滲透壓會變小

(E) 放入丙溶液後，植物細胞膨壓會變大

50. 某植物為短日照植物（長夜性植物），其臨界夜長為8 小時，且需最少三天達臨界夜長後方可開花。下列哪些實驗條件經連續施行四天後，此植物會開花？各選項為實驗期間每天的光照調控情形，每1小格代表1小時，白色方格為照光時段，灰色方格為黑暗時段。（應選3項）

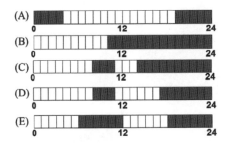

51. 圖16為某種參與「專一性防禦」的細胞，於活化前及活化後，細胞形態變化的示意圖。下列有關該種細胞的敘述，何者正確？

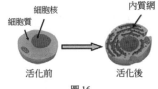

圖 16

(A) 可釋放組織胺，增加血管的通透性

(B) 可釋放血小板，幫助受傷的組織凝血

(C) 可釋放與過敏反應有關的抗體

(D) 為愛滋病病毒（HIV）主要之攻擊對象

(E) 可直接吞噬病原體或受感染的細胞

52. 圖17為甲～丁四人，「ABO血型」及「Rh血型」血液凝集測試結果示意圖。Rh血型以「＋／－」表示，會表現Rh基因者以「＋」標示；反之，則以「－」標示。例如圖中「甲」的血型為B⁺，表示其為B血型並會表現Rh基因。請據以推論乙、丙及丁三人之血型。

(A) 乙－A⁻，丙－B⁺，丁－AB⁻

(B) 乙－A⁺，丙－O⁻，丁－AB⁺

(C) 乙－AB⁺，丙－A⁻，丁－O⁺

(D) 乙－O⁺，丙－A⁻，丁－AB⁻

(E) 乙－O⁺，丙－AB⁻，丁－A⁻

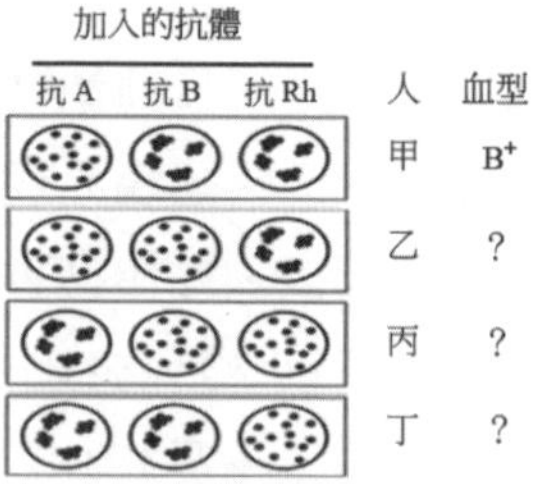

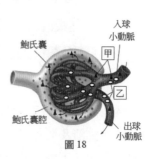

圖 17

53. 圖18為局部腎元構造之示意圖，「甲」和「乙」為血液中的兩類成分。下列選項，何者正確？

	甲	乙
(A)	紅血球	尿素
(B)	尿素	紅血球
(C)	葡萄糖	鈉離子
(D)	鈉離子	葡萄糖
(E)	紅血球	白血球

圖 18

54. 舊金山（39°N）和大西洋城（37°N）分別位於北美洲西岸及東岸，
兩地均濱海而且緯度相近，夏季七月兩地平均之天氣資料如表三
所示：

表三

天氣資料＼地點	舊金山	大西洋城
最高氣溫	18℃	29℃
最低氣溫	12℃	19℃
露點	12℃	18℃
降雨	0.25 mm	94.49 mm
盛行風	西北風	東南風
海水表面溫度	12℃	21℃

下列有關夏季七月兩地平均天氣之敘述，哪些選項正確？
（應選2項）

(A) 舊金山的夜間或清晨較容易出現霧或層雲

(B) 大西洋城單位體積的空氣含水氣量比舊金山較少，所以相對
溼度較低

(C) 大陸高氣壓是夏季七月美洲大陸上的主要天氣系統

(D) 大西洋城的夏季降雨易受東南風與沿岸暖流的影響

(E) 舊金山的天氣主要受到太平洋東北邊低氣壓系統之影響

55. 恆星的光度與其球狀的「表面積」成正比，並且與其「表面溫度
四次方」成正比。已知織女星的絕對星等為0.0、表面溫度為
10,000 K，太陽的絕對星等為5.0、表面溫度為6,000 K。織女星的
半徑大約是太陽的幾倍？

(A) 1.2　　　(B) 3.6　　　(C) 7.7　　　(D) 10　　　(E) 100

56. 海洋中的某些物理、化學特性及生物分布情形不容易直接被觀測到，常常需要藉助儀器的幫助。下列哪些選項可以利用聲納原理測得？（應選2項）
    (A) 海底地形　　　　(B) 海水溫度　　　　(C) 海水鹽度
    (D) 海水溶氧量　　　(E) 海中魚群

請閱讀下列短文後，回答第57-58題

　　碳循環主要是指碳元素在地球的大氣圈、生物圈、水圈及岩石圈等儲存庫之間的交互作用：生物透過光合作用與呼吸作用，使碳於大氣圈及生物圈之間循環；因二氧化碳在水中的溶解度變化，使二氧化碳在大氣圈與水圈之間交換；而在海洋中的沉積物經成岩作用可以將碳儲存至岩石圈；火山作用又可將岩石圈中的碳釋出至大氣圈；而鈣、鎂矽酸鹽類岩石的化學風化作用需使用大氣中的二氧化碳為反應物來分解岩石。碳元素在碳儲存庫之間的交互作用是一種動態平衡的關係。所以在不同的地質年代，大氣中的二氧化碳濃度會呈現不同的變化。

57. 圖19為地球科學家根據不同年代岩石中的相關化學成分，由全球尺度的觀點，推論顯生元以來至工業革命之前，地球大氣中二氧化碳濃度的變化情形。下列哪些選項與圖中曲線變化的關聯性最為密切？（應選2項）

    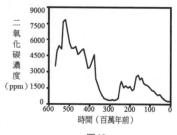
    圖19

    (A) 太陽光度的增加與減少
    (B) 岩石風化速率的增加與減少
    (C) 石灰岩沉積速率的增加與減少
    (D) 陸地植物與動物多樣性的增加與減少
    (E) 大氣中水氣含量及雲量的增加與減少

58. 現今的全球暖化問題,主要是下列哪一因素所造成?

    (A) 火山作用頻率減少

    (B) 風化作用速率增加

    (C) 人類栽種植物面積增加

    (D) 可溶解於海洋中的二氧化碳含量增加

    (E) 埋藏於地層中的有機物質快速減少並氧化

59-60為題組

    化學元素週期表的前三週期如下表所示。已知原子序1-18的元素,其第一主層原子軌域可填入2個電子,第二主層原子軌域可填入8個電子,第三主層原子軌域可填入8個電子。甲與乙為下列週期表中的兩元素。甲原子的最外兩主層的電子數均為2,乙原子為地殼中主要的元素之一,其最外主層電子數是次外主層電子數的3倍。

1 H								2 He
3 Li	4 Be		5 B	6 C	7 N	8 O	9 F	10 Ne
11 Na	12 Mg		13 Al	14 Si	15 P	16 S	17 Cl	18 Ar

    根據上文所述,並參考所附之週期表,回答下列59-60題。

59. 下列何者為甲元素?

    (A) Li   (B) Na   (C) C   (D) Be   (E) Mg

60. 已知由甲、乙兩元素所構成的化合物,在常溫常壓時為固體。下列敘述何者正確?

(A) 元素乙屬於鹵素族　　　　　(B) 元素乙的電子數為4

(C) 元素甲與乙組成的化合物為MgO

(D) 元素甲與乙組成的化合物為$MgCl_2$

(E) 元素甲與乙組成的化合物屬於離子化合物

61. 碳與氧可形成兩種不同的化合物，這兩種化合物中碳和氧的質量比不同。若將碳的質量固定時，兩化合物中氧的質量之間成一簡單整數比，此稱為倍比定律。下列各組物質，何者符合倍比定律？

(A) C_{60}、C_{80}　　　　　(B) Pb_3O_4、PbO　　　　　(C) SiO_2、CO_2

(D) $GaCl_3$、$AlCl_3$　　　　(E) $Al(OH)_3$、Al_2O_3

<u>62-63為題組</u>

　　甲、乙、丙為三種不同濃度的鹽酸溶液，將不同體積的甲、乙、丙溶液分別和<u>過量</u>的強鹼水溶液混合，反應後之總體積皆為10毫升。在反應完全後，所測得溶液之溫度變化（ΔT）如圖20所示：

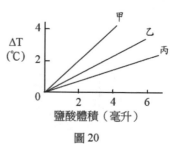

圖 20

62. 下列有關上述反應的敘述，何者<u>錯誤</u>？

(A) 反應後，水溶液的溫度都升高

(B) 反應後，水溶液的pH值都大於7.0

(C) 由反應可推知，此過量的強鹼水溶液為氫氧化鈉水溶液

(D) 反應前，甲、乙與丙三種鹽酸溶液的濃度大小順序為：甲＞乙＞丙

(E) 反應前，若甲溶液的體積為4毫升，則反應後溫度約可增高4℃

63. 根據圖20，約多少毫升的甲溶液與過量的強鹼水溶液反應後，其所產生之溫度變化，相當於5毫升的乙溶液與過量的強鹼水溶液反應，所產生的溫度變化？

　　(A) 1　　　　(B) 2　　　　(C) 3　　　　(D) 4　　　　(E) 5

64-65題爲題組

　　由離地相同高度處，於同一瞬間，使甲球與乙球自靜止狀態開始落下，兩球在抵達地面前，除重力外，只受到來自空氣阻力 F 的作用，此阻力與球的下墜速度 v 成正比，即 $F = -kv\,(k>0)$，且兩球的比例常數 k 完全相同，圖21所示爲兩球的速度-時間關係圖。

64. 若甲球與乙球的質量分別爲 m_1 與 m_2，則下列敘述何者正確？

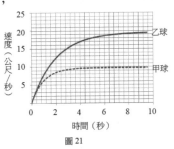

圖21

　　(A) $m_1 = m_2$，且兩球同時抵達地面
　　(B) $m_2 > m_1$，且乙球先抵達地面
　　(C) $m_2 < m_1$，且乙球先抵達地面
　　(D) $m_2 < m_1$，且兩球同時抵達地面
　　(E) $m_2 > m_1$，且甲球先抵達地面

65. 若已知甲球質量爲0.2公斤，落下過程中重力加速度恆爲10公尺/秒^2，則比例常數 k 值約爲多少公斤/秒？

　　(A) 0.1　　　(B) 0.2　　　(C) 4　　　(D) 10　　　(E) 40

66. 棒球比賽中，打擊者用力向斜上方揮棒，擊出高飛全壘打。若不考慮空氣阻力，因此棒球在空中飛行時水平方向不受外力作用，則下列圖形何者可以代表棒球的水平方向速度 v_x 與其落地前飛行時間 t 的關係？

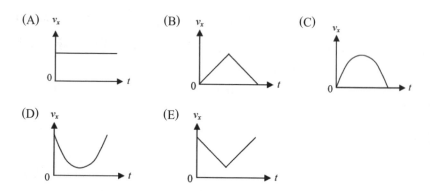

67. 跳遠比賽時，某生助跑後從起跳板躍起落在沙坑中，已知起跳點與落地點在同一水平面。若空氣阻力可忽略，跳遠者僅受重力作用且可視為質量集中於質心的質點，則在該生起跳後到落地前的過程中，下列有關其運動的敘述哪些是正確的？（應選2項）

(A) 該生作等速度運動

(B) 該生作等加速度運動

(C) 該生作變速圓周運動

(D) 該生的速率在最高點達最大

(E) 該生落地前的瞬間速率等於躍起時的瞬間速率

68. 甲、乙兩容器中間以附有閘門的狹管相連，閘門關閉時，體積為20公升的甲容器內裝有3.0大氣壓的氮氣，體積為40公升的乙容器內裝有6.0大氣壓的空氣，兩容器的氣體溫度均為300 K。閘門打開後兩容器氣體開始混合，並且將混合後氣體的溫度加熱至420 K。若兩容器與狹管的體積不隨溫度而變，則平衡後容器內混合氣體的壓力為幾大氣壓？

(A) 3.0　　　(B) 4.0　　　(C) 5.0　　　(D) 6.0　　　(E) 7.0

101年度學科能力測驗自然科試題詳解

第壹部分

一、單選題

1. **D**

　　【解析】　依課文敘述，細胞膜構造如下圖所示：

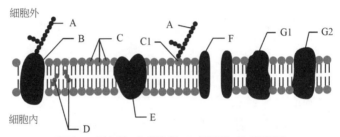

A-醣類、B-蛋白質、C-磷脂質、D-膽固醇、E-受體蛋白
F-溝道蛋白、G1-被動運輸載體蛋白、G2-主動運輸載體蛋白

　　　所以細胞膜的成分不包含去氧核醣核酸，故答案選 (D)

2. **C**

　　【解析】　丙構造為細胞板，出現於有絲分裂末期，所以不應出
　　　　　現於有絲分裂後期，故答案選 (C)

3-4 為題組

3. **A**

　　【解析】　本題不應考慮子代數量，考慮基因型種類即可，基因
　　　　　型種類越少，對環境適應能力越差，因疾病而滅絕的
　　　　　可能性越大，故此題選 (A)

4. **E**

【解析】 根據題意病原體爲病毒，故

(A) 病毒可利用寄主細胞合成蛋白質

(B) 病毒無有性生殖

(C) 植物病毒爲 RNA 病毒，細菌病毒－噬菌體爲 DNA 病毒，動物病毒爲 DNA 或 RNA 病毒

(D) 病毒不可能同時兼具 DNA 及 RNA

(E) 病毒獨自存在時不具有任何生命現象，故此題答案選 (E)

5-6 爲題組

5. **A**

【解析】 根據圖示，乙、丙、丁具有單一食性均捕食甲，故競爭較爲激烈，此題答案選 (A)

6. **C**

【解析】 戊物種滅絕時，族群受到影響而增長的物種爲乙、丙、丁，乙物種被己、辛捕食，丙物種被己捕食，丁物種被己、庚捕食，故最直接快速增長的物種選丙

7. **D**

【解析】 根據圖示，甲：年雨量最低，爲沙漠生態系；乙、丙年均溫高皆高，而乙雨量適中爲落葉闊葉林生態系，丙雨量降多爲熱帶雨林生態系；丁年均溫在 0℃ 上下雨量適中，爲針葉林生態系；戊年雨量及溫度均偏低，爲苔原生態系，故此題答案選 (D)

8. **D**

【解析】 依圖形可判斷出 X 魚種適合生長的溫度範圍 20～30
（℃），鹽度為 18～23（千分之一）；Y 魚種適合生長的
溫度範圍 20～25(℃)，鹽度為 28～33（千分之一），
故 X 物種可在丙、丁養殖池飼養，Y 物種可在甲養殖
池飼養，此題答案選 (D)

9. **D**

【解析】 星雲發出的光很微弱，僅可能在銀河系內才能被觀測
到，因此 M42 為於銀河系內。渦狀星系是銀河系外與
銀河系大小相近的星系。因此 M31 距離較遠。故答案
選 (D)

10. **D**

【解析】 古時候對於恆星與行星的定義，在於一個會動，一個
不會動。相對位置不變的為恆星，相對位置改變的稱
為行星。故答案選 (D)

11. **D**

【解析】 (A) 隱沒帶是海洋地殼的最外圍，距離中洋脊最遠的
　　　　地方。因此年齡最老

　　　(B) 錯誤

　　　(C) 隱沒帶屬於聚合型的板塊邊界

　　　(D) 岩石圈＝板塊，隱沒帶就是岩石圈向下往軟流圈
　　　　靠近。正確

　　　(E) 地震波傳遞的方向為球狀，不是單一方向傳遞

12. **A**

【解析】 (A) 正確

(B) 不是僅有順向波才會發生山崩

(C) 山崩與岩石性質沒有絕對關係

(D) 無關

(E) 無法完全阻止山崩

13. **E**

【解析】 僅考慮科氏力，北半球科氏力垂直運動方向往右邊作用，中央附近水位最高。但本題顯然與自然現象旋轉產生離心力導致中央水位較低不符

14. **D**

【解析】 (A) 一般而言海洋表面因為生物群聚的關係，營養鹽較少

(B) 下層海水密度較大，此時處於穩定的狀態不易對流。因此不會混合

(C) 二氧化碳含量一般隨深度增加

(D) 由於海水不混合，因此僅有表層有光合作用，底部含氧量較低，正確

(E) 不一定

15. **E**

【解析】 (A) 溫度越低，飽和水氣壓越小

(B) 溫度越低，空氣密度越大

(C) 題目敘述 2 地氣壓相同

(D) 溫度越低，水氣達到飽和的溫度（露點溫度）越低

(E) 空氣密度越大，地面附近氣壓變化率越大。故選 (E)

16. **E**

【解析】 (A) 赤道附近的信風會增強

(B) 湧升流變強

(C) 赤道附近東側海水水溫降低

(D) 氣壓在太平洋赤道附近為西高東低

(E) 正確

17. **D**

【解析】 (甲)(乙) 皆正確

(丙) 化學技術合成新的分子或是聚合物，本項無誤

(丁) 天然有機食物仍為化合物

(戊) 輕油裂解技術仍是依賴化石燃料為主能源

18. **D**

【解析】 1 莫耳無水乙醇完全燃燒可產生 2 莫耳二氧化碳

又 $CO_2 + Ca(OH)_2 \rightarrow CaCO_3 + H_2O$

$\Rightarrow$ 由此可推知此無水乙醇為 $\dfrac{0.1}{2} = 0.05\,\text{mole}$

0.05mole 放出熱量 Q，1mole 放出熱量 $\dfrac{1}{0.05}Q = 20Q$

19. **B**

【解析】 由題幹，此物需為中性電解質 $\Rightarrow$ (C)(D)(E)不合

又需與 CO_3^{2-}、OH^- 沉澱 $\Rightarrow$ 僅氯化鈣符合

20. **B**

【解析】 (A)(C) 由圖 5 可知，H_2O 的生成為放熱反應

(D) 為放熱反應

(E) 為吸熱反應

21. **A**

【解析】(甲) $\Rightarrow x-t$ 圖的斜率等於速度

而甲圖是斜直線 $\Rightarrow$ 斜率固定 $\Rightarrow$ 速度固定

$\Rightarrow$ 加速度 $a_甲 = 0$

(乙) $v-t$ 圖斜率等於加速度

5 秒時，乙圖斜率 = 0 $\Rightarrow$ 加速度 $a_乙 = 0$

(丙) 由 $a-t$ 圖 $\Rightarrow a_丙 = 0.2$

∴丙＞甲＝乙

22. **E**

【解析】(A) 繩索拉回的過程

(B) 同上，人向上加速的過程

(C) 落下過程

(D) 同 (A)，繩子無拉力，人上昇減速的過程

23. **C**

【解析】已知靜電力為兩電荷間作用力與反作用力

故 $F_{PHe} = F_{HeP} = F$

24. **B**

【解析】水密度較空氣大

但強度↓（能量損失）

頻率不變

波速 ↗（$v_固 > v_液 > v_氣$）

波長 ↗（由 $v = f\lambda$，$v \propto \lambda$）

方向偏向法線（由司乃爾定律）

25. **B**

【解析】 因太空中無介質，故熱靠輻射傳出

26. **D**

【解析】 由安培右手定則，甲乙丙三線圈，磁極方向相同，故互相吸引

27-28 為題組

27. **B**

【解析】 由 $\dfrac{V_1}{n_1} = \dfrac{V_2}{n_2}$　$\dfrac{6000}{3} = \dfrac{V_2}{200} \Rightarrow V_2 = 4 \times 10^5$

28. **A**

【解析】 由輸出功率 $W = IV$，則 $V \searrow$，$I \nearrow$

導線消耗功率 $W = I_2 R \propto I_2$

則 $\dfrac{W'}{W} = \dfrac{I'^2}{I^2} = \dfrac{V^2}{V'^2} = \dfrac{n^2}{n'^2} = \dfrac{200^2}{100^2} = 4$

二、多選題

29. **AE**

【解析】 (A) 複式顯微鏡接目鏡及接物鏡均為可聚光、具有放大效果的凸透鏡

(B) 光源由載物臺下方向上，先經過生物切片才進入接物鏡

(C) 觀察生切片時應該先以低倍鏡觀察，低倍鏡視野較大，利於尋找物體

(D) 當接物鏡由 4 倍換到 40 倍，直線倍率放大 10 倍，視野下直線距離減為 1/10 倍，面積則減為原來面積的 1/100 倍

(E) 顯微鏡放大倍率為接目鏡倍率×接物鏡倍率，故 5×40 與 10×20 均為 200 倍，兩者放大倍率相同，故此題答案選 (A)(E)

30. **DE**

【解析】 海帶－褐藻（原生生物界），玉米－單子葉植物（植物界），鳥巢蕨－蕨類（植物界），香菇－蕈類（真菌界），酵母菌－真菌（真菌界），番茄－雙子葉植物（植物界），四季豆－雙子葉植物（植物界），石花菜－紅藻（原生生物界），故此題答案選 (D)(E)

31. **ABD**

【解析】 (A) 湧升流帶來較冷的海水，導致海陸的氣溫差異加大。白天海風更為明顯。正確

(B) 湧升流帶來較冷的海水，空氣溫度降低，導致飽和成霧。正確

(C) 底部水密度較高，湧升流發生的位置表面海水的密度較大，錯誤

(D) 湧升流帶來較冷的海水。正確

(E) 溶氧量與湧升流無關。錯誤

32. **ACE**

【解析】 (B)(D) 的事件發生在生命誕生之後，不在 40 億年前

33. **CD**

【解析】 (A) 不一定　　(B) 錯誤　　(C) 正確　　(E) 錯誤

(D) 午後陸地上升氣流旺盛，海風最強。正確

34. **CD**

【解析】 共價鍵 ⇒ 非金屬與非金屬進行鍵結 ⇒ 故選 (C) (D)

35. **AD**

【解析】 (B) 以氯化鈉的導電性最好

(C) 氯化鈉的熔點為最高

(E) 乙醇才是揮發性有機溶劑

36. **AC**

【解析】 (B) 人類無法消化纖維素

(D) 葡萄糖為單醣（分子式 $C_6H_{12}O_6$），寡醣為 $3-9$ 個單醣脫水而成，故分子較葡萄糖大；但因寡醣對人體仍算小分子，故可被人體吸收

(E) 蔗糖為雙醣，1 分子蔗糖＝1 分子葡萄糖＋1 分子果糖，並脫去一分子的水

37. **AE**

【解析】 (A) $H_2 + CuO \rightarrow Cu + H_2O$

(B) $CO + O_2 \rightarrow CO_2$（後方無單一元素的物質）

(C) $CO + CuO \rightarrow Cu + CO_2$（前方無單一元素的物質）

(D) $Ag + CuSO_4 \rightarrow \times$

(E) $Zn + CuSO_4 \rightarrow Cu + ZnSO_4$

38. **BD**

【解析】 (A) 在甲管中是 Ca^{2+} 與 Na^+ 交換

(C) 是 SO_4^{2-} 與 OH^- 交換

(E) 使用氫氧化鈉再生

39. **BD**

【解析】 (A) (D) 陰極附近溶液為鹼性

(B) 電解 KI 陽極反應：$2I^- \rightarrow I_2，I_2 + I^- \rightarrow I_3^-$

(C) H_2

(E) 正己烷和水分層，正己烷密度較小在上層，水在下層，因為溶入碘分子，故呈現紫色

40. **BE**

【解析】 同分異構物 ⇒ 分子式相同，結構不同

(A) O_2、O_3 互為同素異型體

(D) 蛋白質為胺基酸聚合物，耐綸為己二胺和己二酸聚合物，兩者分子式不同

(C) 金剛石與 C_{60} 為同素異型體

41. **DE**

【解析】 (D) 電漿不是

(E) 液晶不是

42. **BD**

【解析】 色散 ⇒ 多色光＋折射鏡

43. **CE**

【解析】 由司乃爾定律

水 → 空氣，密度↓ ⇒ 偏離法線(丙)

空氣 → 水，密度↑ ⇒ 作向法線(己)

三、綜合題

44. **E**

【解析】 Y 段 DNA 旋轉 360°，包含 10 對鹼基對，共有 20 個含氮鹼基，故此題答案選 (E)

45. **D**

【解析】 DNA 鹼基配對中，A 與 T 以兩個氫鍵配對，C 與 G 以三個氫鍵配對，題目序列中包含 4 個 A，4 個 T，6 個 C，6 個 G，共 8 組 A：T 配對，12 組 C：G 配對，含 $8 \times 2 + 12 \times 3 = 52$ 個氫鍵，故此題答案選 (D)

46. **E**

【解析】 X 光無法穿透地球大氣，因此必須在地球的大氣層外觀測。范艾輪輻射帶為高能帶電粒子密集處，不適合放置望遠鏡，因此答案選 (E)

47. **C**

【解析】 (A) $(210-84)-(226-88)=126-138=-12$

(B) $84-88=-4$

(C) ∵質子數＝電子數　∴差 4

(D) 都存在，很早便有人研究

(E) 來自原子核的衰變，會放出 α、β、γ 射線但沒有 X 光

48. **C**

【解析】 超音波：利用音波透射進入人體，遇觀測物之後反射
回來

內視鏡：將胃腸中的影像經由光纖全反射傳回儀器判讀

放射線：利用原子核衰變產生之 γ 射線作為殺死癌細胞
之工具

X　光：原子中之電子由激發態躍回較低能態時，會將
能量以電磁波之形式放出

第貳部分

49. **AD**

【解析】 依圖示可判斷出植物細胞置於甲溶液後較為膨脹，置於
乙溶液後無明顯變化，置於丙溶液後原生質萎縮，故三
蔗糖溶液濃度為：丙＞乙＞甲，而植物細胞置於濃度最
低的甲溶液中，細胞外水份滲入植物細胞多，故膨壓最
大，且因水份進入細胞中增加，使細胞濃度降低滲透壓
變小；而細胞置於乙溶液中無明顯變化代表進入細胞的
水份與出細胞的水份相等，維持動態平衡；而細胞置於
丙溶液中水份滲出細胞過多，細胞膜與細胞壁分離產生
質離現象，膨壓為零，故此題答案選 (A) (D)

50. **ABC**

【解析】 已知此短日照植物的臨界夜長為 8 小時，故只要連續黑
夜達到或長於 8 小時處理之下此植物均可開花，且需注
意選項中圖形 24 小時之後是接續下一日的 0 小時，而
(A) 連續 9 小時黑夜，(B) 連續 14 小時黑夜，(C) 連續 10
小時黑夜，故此題答案選 (A) (B) (C)

51. **C**

【解析】　依照圖示，活化後細胞粗糙內質網增生可判斷出此細胞
　　　　　要製造蛋白質，而五個選項中只有 (C) 抗體為蛋白質，
　　　　　故此題答案選 (C)

52. **D**

【解析】　與抗 A 抗體凝集的為 A 型，與抗 B 抗體凝集的為 B 型，
　　　　　與抗 A 及抗 B 抗體均凝集的為 AB 型，與抗 A 及抗 B 抗
　　　　　體均不凝集的為 O 型，與抗 Rh 抗體凝集的代表 Rh$^+$，
　　　　　與抗 Rh 抗體不凝集的代表 Rh$^-$，故此題答案選 (D)

53. **B**

【解析】　由圖形可知甲物質可擴散出微血管進入鮑氏囊，故必不
　　　　　為血球，乙物質不可擴散出鮑氏囊，故必為血球，此題
　　　　　答案選 (B)

54. **AD**

【解析】　(A) 露點溫度較低處較容易出現霧，正確
　　　　　(B) 由雨量大致可以判斷大西洋城較潮濕
　　　　　(C) 錯誤
　　　　　(D) 正確
　　　　　(E) 錯誤

55. **B**

【解析】　0 等星與 5 等的亮度差 100 倍

　　　　　$(10000/6000)^4 = 7.72$

　　　　　表面積 $= 4\pi r^2$

　　　　　$(3.6)^2 \times 7.72 = 100$

　　　　　因此織女星的半徑約為太陽的 3.6 倍左右

56. **AE**

【解析】 聲納必須碰到物體才有回波，因此答案選(A)(E)

57-58 為題組

57. **BC**

【解析】 由題目敘述可知答案為 (B)(C)

58. **E**

【解析】 人類燃燒化石燃料導致二氧化碳含量上升，是全球暖化的主因。故答案選 (E)

59-60 為題組

59. **D**

【解析】 Be 的電子組態為 $1s^2 2s^2$，電子數排列 (2,2)

60. **E**

【解析】 (A) 電子數排列為 (2,6)，故乙為氧元素，屬於氧族

(B) 電子數為 8

(C)(D) 為 BeO

61. **B**

【解析】 倍比定律成立在相同兩元素構成的化合物，其固定化合物中其中一元素質量，另一元素質量成最簡整數比

<u>62-63 為題組</u>

62. **C**

【解析】(A) 由圖可知，$\Delta T = T_2 - T_1 =$ 正值，溫度皆上升

(B) 題幹為「過量強鹼」，故水溶液 pH 值＞7

(C) 無法得知

(D) 由圖可知，同體積下放出的熱量為甲＞乙＞丙，

故可推知酸的濃度為甲＞乙＞丙

(E) 由圖可知，正確

63. **C**

【解析】由圖可知，約 3mol 的甲溶液升溫和 5mol 的乙溶液

相同

<u>64-65 為題組</u>

64. **B**

【解析】由原題式子 $F = -kv$ 可知 $|F| \propto |v|$

則達終端速度時，合力為零，則 $F = mg$

$\therefore |F| \propto |v| \propto m$ $\quad \therefore m_2 > m_1$

又 $v-t$ 圖面積等於位移

$\therefore$ 乙球先落地

65. **B**

【解析】由圖中甲的終端速度為 10m/s 向下

$F = -kv = mg \Rightarrow 0.2 \times 10 = -k \times (-10) \Rightarrow k = 0.2$

66. **A**

【解析】 斜向拋射時，水平方向不受外力 ⇒ 做等速度運動
⇒ (A)

67. **BE**

【解析】 (A) 速度方向有變 ⇒ 非等速

(B) 僅有重力加速度 g

(C) 拋物線，非圓周運動

(D) 最小（僅有水平速度）

(E) 力學能守恆（$\Delta k = -\Delta U = 0$）

68. **E**

【解析】 由 $PV = nRT$

原甲室 $P_1 V_1 = n_1 R T_1 \Rightarrow 3 \times 20 = n_1 R 300 \Rightarrow n_1 = \dfrac{1}{5R}$

原乙室 $P_2 V_2 = n_2 R T_2 \Rightarrow 6 \times 40 = n_2 R 300 \Rightarrow n_2 = \dfrac{4}{5R}$

混合後 $P'V' = n'RT'$

$P' \times (20 + 40) = (n_1 + n_2) R \times 420$

$\Rightarrow P' \times 60 = (\dfrac{1}{5R} + \dfrac{4}{5R}) R \times 420$

$\Rightarrow P' = 7$

101 年大學入學學科能力測驗試題 國文考科

第壹部分：選擇題（佔 54 分）

一、單選題（佔 30 分）

說明：第 1 題至第 15 題，每題有 4 個選項，其中只有一個是正確或最適當的選項，請畫記在答案卡之「選擇題答案區」。各題答對者，得 2 分；答錯、未作答或畫記多於一個選項者，該題以零分計算。

1. 下列各組「」內的字，讀音相同的選項是：
   (A) 「佚」名／瓜「瓞」綿綿
   (B) 「呀」然／驚「訝」不已
   (C) 「鶼」鰈／「鬮」然媚世
   (D) 地「氈」／「饘」粥糊口

2. 下列文句中，完全沒有錯別字的選項是：
   (A) 教育下一代最好的方法就是父母要以身作責
   (B) 不肖商人利慾薰心，竟將塑化劑摻入果汁中販售
   (C) 在老師提綱切領的說明之後，所有問題都獲得解答
   (D) 公司仍在草創階段，人力短缺，經費不足，只好因漏就簡

3. 詞語中有一種結構是「名詞＋名詞」，其中前者用來說明後者的功用，如「垃圾車」。下列具有此種修飾方式的選項是：
   (A) 牛肉麵　　　　　　　　(B) 水果刀
   (C) 老爺車　　　　　　　　(D) 鵝蛋臉

4. 下列文句「」內成語的運用,正確的選項是:

(A) 下課鐘聲一響,小朋友就如「新鶯出谷」般地衝出教室

(B) 縱有「鬼斧神工」的本領,也無法改變人生無常的事實

(C) 社區居民來自不同省分,說起話來猶如「郢書燕說」,南腔北調

(D) 閱讀古籍如碰到「郭公夏五」的情況,必須多方查考,力求正確

5. 閱讀下文,依序選出最適合填入□□內的選項:

甲、小個子繼續跑,我繼續追;激湍的河面□□著一線白光,很像是球,在另一端與我競速賽跑。(張啓疆〈消失的球〉)

乙、那段日子裡,每當我的思念□□得將要潰堤時,竟是書中許多句子和意象安慰我、幫助我平靜下來。(李黎〈星沉海底〉)

丙、此刻,我獨自一人,□□對望雨洗過的蒼翠山巒與牛奶般柔細的煙嵐,四顧茫茫,樹下哪裡還有花格子衣的人影?(陳義芝〈爲了下一次的重逢〉)

(A) 浮滾/洶湧/蕭索　　　(B) 映照/沖刷/悠然

(C) 浮滾/沖刷/蕭索　　　(D) 映照/洶湧/悠然

6. 甲、咬牙切齒/就代表我和你的親密關係

乙、我擁有各式大小橫直的數字/電腦計算機總算不清這筆賬/我沒有生命/但/收拾生命

丙、美味是早天的原罪/肉身卸甲之後/無防備地讓蒜泥調情調味/下酒/並且消化/在人體裡留下膽固醇的伏筆/以在對方無可抵禦的老年/溫柔地報復

上述三首詩所描寫的對象依序是:

(A) 拉鍊/電話/扇貝　　　(B) 鋸子/日曆/扇貝

(C) 拉鍊/日曆/螃蟹　　　(D) 鋸子/電話/螃蟹

7. 下列□□中的詞語，依序最適合填入的選項是：

甲、近自海外旅遊歸來，特選購當地名產乙盒，敬希□□

乙、來訪未晤，因有要事相商，明早十時再趨拜，務請□□爲幸

丙、茲訂於元月十七日下午六時，敬備□□，恭候光臨

(A) 哂納／賜見／菲酌

(B) 拜收／稍待／嘉禮

(C) 笑納／曲留／華筵

(D) 惠存／恭候／賀儀

8. 下列是一段古文，請依文意選出排列順序最恰當的選項：

《大學》之書，古之大學所以教人之法也。蓋自天降生民，

甲、然其氣質之禀或不能齊

乙、則天必命之以爲億兆之君師

丙、則既莫不與之以仁義禮智之性矣

丁、一有聰明睿智能盡其性者出於其間

戊、是以不能皆有以知其性之所有而全之也

使之治而教之，以復其性。（朱熹〈大學章句序〉）

(A) 甲戊丙乙丁　　　　　　　(B) 乙丁丙甲戊

(C) 丙甲戊丁乙　　　　　　　(D) 丁乙甲戊丙

9. 下列文句所描寫的景色，依一年時序的先後，排列正確的選項是：

甲、梅英疏淡，冰澌溶洩，東風暗換年華

乙、菡萏香銷翠葉殘，西風愁起綠波間。還與容光共憔悴，不堪看

丙、玉樓明月長相憶，柳絲裊娜春無力。門外草萋萋，送君聞馬嘶

丁、黃菊枝頭生曉寒，人生莫放酒杯乾。風前橫笛斜吹雨，醉裡
　　簪花倒著冠

(A) 甲乙丙丁　　　　　　　　(B) 甲丙乙丁

(C) 丙甲乙丁　　　　　　　　(D) 丙丁乙甲

10. 閱讀以下金庸《射鵰英雄傳》文字，根據文意、情境，依序選出最適合填入_____的選項：

　　黃蓉道：「做這篇文章的范文正公，當年威震西夏，文才武略，可說得上並世無雙。」郭靖央她將范仲淹的事跡說了一些，聽她說到他幼年家貧、父親早死、母親改嫁種種苦況，富貴後儉樸異常，處處為百姓著想，不禁油然起敬，在飯碗中滿滿斟了一碗酒，仰脖子一飲而盡，說道：「_____，大英雄大豪傑固當如此胸懷！」（第26回）

　　黃蓉道：「當面撒謊！你有這許多女人陪你，還寂寞甚麼？」歐陽克張開摺扇，搧了兩搧，雙眼凝視著她，微笑吟道：「_____。」黃蓉向他做個鬼臉，笑道：「我不用你討好，更加不用你思念。」（第12回）

甲、心曠神怡，寵辱偕忘

乙、先天下之憂而憂，後天下之樂而樂

丙、悠悠我心，豈無他人？唯君之故，沉吟至今

丁、日暮長江裏，相邀歸渡頭。落花如有意，來去逐船流

(A) 甲丙　　　　(B) 甲丁　　　　(C) 乙丙　　　　(D) 乙丁

11. 蜀中有杜處士，好書畫，所寶以百數。有戴嵩〈牛〉一軸，尤所愛，錦囊玉軸，常以自隨。一日曝書畫，有一牧童見之，拊掌大笑，曰：「此畫鬥牛也。牛鬥，力在角，尾搐入兩股間。今乃掉尾而鬥，謬矣。」處士笑而然之。古語有云：「耕當問奴，織當問婢。」不可改也。（蘇軾〈書戴嵩畫牛〉）

下列文句與上文主旨最不相關的選項是：

(A) 聞道有先後，術業有專攻

(B) 學無常師，有一業勝己者，便從學焉

(C) 使言之而是，雖在褐夫芻蕘，猶不可棄也

(D) 三人行，必有我師焉。擇其善者而從之，其不善者而改之

12-13為題組

下文是一則記者對林懷民演講內容的報導，閱讀後回答12-13題。

　　林懷民回憶，當初回國到雲門才開始學編舞，一開始就遇到最大的挑戰「如何跳自己的舞。」歐美舞者手一伸、腳一跳，你就能立刻認出背後的文化符號；跳舞和藝術一樣，從來不是中性的，需要歷史和文化長久的涵養。

　　「就像巴黎的印象畫，陽光是透明的。南臺灣的陽光卻是炙熱的，把萬物都曬到模糊；我們卻從來只認得義大利的文化復興、法國的印象派、安迪沃荷的瑪麗蓮夢露。」

　　林懷民指著畫家廖繼春作品「有香蕉樹的院子」，畫中展現南臺灣獨有的陽光、溫度。「就像侯孝賢的悲情城市，空鏡頭裡都是濕氣，把海島國家才有的面貌呈現。」他說，這是技法在服務畫作和生活，「這才是屬於臺灣的藝術。」（鄭語謙〈肉身解嚴〉）

12. 依據上文來看，最切合林懷民創作觀點的選項是：
 (A) 藝術無國界
 (B) 美感素養影響美感體驗
 (C) 藝術創作要與土地結合以呈現特有風貌結
 (D) 歷史文化長久的涵養才能孕育藝術創作

13. 這則報導內容包括四個重點，按其文中呈現的次序，排列最適當的選項是：
 甲、期許自我創作的獨特
 乙、反省藝術教育的限制
 丙、連結其他藝術的創作
 丁、確立藝術發展的方向

 (A) 甲乙丙丁　　　　　　(B) 乙甲丁丙
 (C) 丙丁甲乙　　　　　　(D) 丁丙乙甲

14-15為題組

閱讀方孝孺〈越車〉,回答14-15題。

　　越無車,有遊者得車於晉、楚之郊,輻朽而輪敗,輗折而轅毀,無所可用。然以其鄉之未嘗有也,舟載以歸,而誇諸人。觀者聞其誇而信之,以為車固若是,效而為之者相屬。他日,晉、楚之人見而笑其拙,越人以為紿己,不顧。及寇兵侵其境,越率敝車禦之。車壞,大敗,終不知其車也。

14. 依據上文,下列各句「之」字指「越國遊者所說的話」的選項是:
　　(A) 然以其鄉「之」未嘗有也　　(B) 觀者聞其誇而信「之」
　　(C) 效而為「之」者相屬　　　　(D) 越率敝車禦「之」

15. 依據上文,敘述正確的選項是:
　　(A) 越人以為晉、楚之人所言不實,故對其譏笑不予理睬
　　(B) 越國遊者改造的晉、楚戰車不夠精良,因此被敵寇打敗
　　(C) 越人故意用殘破的戰車與寇兵作戰,使其輕敵,終獲勝利
　　(D) 越國遊者將晉、楚大軍的戰車毀壞,成功地阻止晉、楚入侵

二、多選題(佔 24 分)

說明:　第 16 題至第 23 題,每題有 5 個選項,其中至少有一個是正確的選項,選出正確選項畫記在答案卡之「選擇題答案區」。各題之選項獨立判定,所有選項均答對者,得 3 分;答錯 1 個選項者,得 1.8 分;答錯 2 個選項者,得 0.6 分;答錯多於 2 個選項或所有選項均未作答者,該題以零分計算。

16. 「人怕出名,豬怕肥」是「人怕出名就好像豬怕肥」的意思。有些日常用語,在表達上也具有這樣的比喻意涵。下列屬於相同用法的選項是:

(A) 三天打魚，兩天曬網　　　(B) 一朝被蛇咬，十年怕草繩

(C) 千里送鵝毛，禮輕情意重　(D) 善惡不同途，冰炭不同爐

(E) 強求的愛情不美，強摘的果實不甜

17. 下列關於白靈詩句的解說，正確的選項是：

(A) 「鐘／因謙虛而被敲響」，「謙虛」是形容鐘的中空

(B) 「落日──掉在大海的波浪上／彈了兩下」，表現夕陽沉落時的空間動感

(C) 「黃昏時，天空焚為一座／燦爛的廢墟／落日自高處倒塌」，描寫日全蝕的荒涼景象

(D) 「白蛇似的小溪逐雨聲／一路嬌喘爬來／碰到撐黑傘的松／躲進傘影不見了」，描寫白蛇躲進樹叢的生動情景

(E) 「沙灘上浪花來回印刷了半世紀／那條船再不曾踩上來／斷槳一般成了大海的野餐／老婦人坐在門前，眼裏有一張帆／日日糾纏著遠方」，描寫老婦人等待遠方未歸人的執著

18. 臺灣近五十年來名作家輩出，其中不少作家吸收古典文學之美，融會貫通後，創造出個人獨特的風格。例如詩人　甲　將文化中國當作母親，表現濃厚的鄉愁，在現代詩、現代散文、文學批評及翻譯上也都有相當成就。而　乙　將古典詩詞的語彙和意象融入現代詩的情境當中，一首〈錯誤〉有著典雅細膩的浪漫情調，被人廣為傳誦。至於女作家　丙　、　丁　均善用古典詞語寫出精緻動人的散文，前者多以懷舊憶往的題材為主，在平凡無奇中涵蘊至理，充滿中國倫理色彩；後者寫作風格以多樣著稱，有時細膩溫柔，有時辛辣諷刺，並曾將古典故事改編為現代戲劇。另外，　戊　熱愛中國傳統文化，又嫻熟西方現代主義，曾將崑曲〈牡丹亭〉融入小說〈遊園驚夢〉中。

上文＿＿＿中，依序最適合填入的選項是：

(A) 甲、楊牧　　　　　　　(B) 乙、鄭愁予

(C) 丙、琦君　　　　　　　(D) 丁、張曉風

(E) 戊、白先勇

19. 下列有關文化知識的敘述，正確的選項是：
    (A) 《資治通鑑》為司馬光所撰，以人物傳記為主，屬於「紀傳體」
    (B) 〈項脊軒志〉的「志」即「記」，該篇重點在記錄書齋建造的原因及過程
    (C) 〈左忠毅公軼事〉中的「軼事」又稱「逸事」，多屬史傳沒有記載且不為人知之事
    (D) 《儒林外史》揭露儒林群相的醜態，是一部詳細記載中國科舉制度的重要史書
    (E) 《臺灣通史》起自隋代，終於割讓，是研究臺灣歷史的重要典籍

20. 下列各組文句，「」內字義相同的選項是：
    (A) 後「值」傾覆，受任於敗軍之際／復「值」接輿醉，狂歌五柳前
    (B) 軒凡四遭火，得不焚，「殆」有神護者／學而不思則罔，思而不學則「殆」
    (C) 況陽春召我以煙景，大塊「假」我以文章／願「假」東壁輝，餘光照貧女
    (D) 梁使三反，孟嘗君「固」辭不往也／彼眾昏之日，「固」未嘗無獨醒之人也
    (E) 「庸」奴！此何地也？而汝來前／吾師道也，夫「庸」知其年之先後生於吾乎

21. 文學作品中，常採用「由大而小」及「由遠而近」的手法，逐漸聚焦到所要描寫的重點對象。下列同時使用此兩種手法的選項是：
    (A) 平林漠漠煙如織，寒山一帶傷心碧。暝色入高樓，有人樓上愁
    (B) 枯藤老樹昏鴉，小橋流水人家，古道西風瘦馬，夕陽西下，斷腸人在天涯

(C) 寸寸柔腸，盈盈粉淚，樓高莫近危闌倚。平蕪盡處是春山，
行人更在春山外

(D) 畫閣魂銷，高樓目斷，斜陽只送平波遠。無窮無盡是離愁，
天涯地角尋思遍

(E) 青青河畔草，鬱鬱園中柳。盈盈樓上女，皎皎當窗牖，娥娥
紅粉妝，纖纖出素手

22. 古典詩中的「月亮」在不同情境之下，有不同的意涵。下列詩句
藉「月」來抒發「思婦懷人」之情的選項是：

(A) 戍鼓斷人行，邊秋一雁聲。露從今夜白，月是故鄉明

(B) 霜威出塞早，雲色渡河秋。夢繞邊城月，心飛故國樓

(C) 鶯啼燕語報新年，馬邑龍堆路幾千。家住秦城鄰漢苑，心隨
明月到胡天

(D) 可憐樓上月徘徊，應照離人妝鏡臺。玉戶簾中捲不去，搗衣
砧上拂還來

(E) 白狼河北音書斷，丹鳳城南秋夜長。誰為含愁獨不見，更教
明月照流黃

23. 閱讀下文，選出敘述正確的選項：

　　余昔少年讀書，竊嘗怪顏子以簞食瓢飲，居於陋巷，人不堪其
憂，顏子不改其樂。私以為雖不欲仕，然抱關擊柝尚可自養，而不
害於學，何至困辱貧窶自苦如此？及來筠州，勤勞鹽米之間，無一
日之休，雖欲棄塵垢，解羈縶，自放於道德之場，而事每劫而留之。
然後知顏子之所以甘心貧賤，不肯求斗升之祿以自給者，良以其害
於學故也。（蘇轍〈東軒記〉）

(A) 作者來到筠州之後，生活和顏回一樣貧窮艱困

(B) 俗世塵垢使作者深受羈絆，因而渴望擺脫俗務干擾

(C) 作者年少時認為：從事抱關擊柝的工作並不妨礙學習

(D) 由於親身經驗，作者終於明瞭顏回之所以不仕，是想全心致力為學

(E) 作者從小對顏回「簞食瓢飲，居於陋巷」而「不改其樂」的生活，就頗為欣賞

第貳部分：非選擇題（共三大題，佔 54 分）

說明：請依各題指示作答，答案務必寫在「答案卷」上，並標明題號一、二、三。

一、文章解讀（佔 9 分）

閱讀框內文章之後，請解讀：為什麼作者認為「心教」才是劍橋教育真正的精華？並加以評論。文長約150—200字（約7—9行）。

> 　　劍橋的教育，最有作用的恐怕不在「言教」。其導修制，是在「言教」之外，還有「身教」，這一向被視為劍橋的特色。這點是真，但也不可太過誇張，依我想，劍橋的「心教」也許才是真正的精華。「心教」是每個人對景物的孤寂中的晤對，是每個人對永恆的剎那間的捕捉。劍橋的偉大之子，不論是大詩人或大科學家，對宇宙人生都有那種晤對與捕捉。劍橋的教育似乎特別重視一景一物的營造，在他們看來，教室、實驗室固然是教育的場所，但一石之擺置、一花之鋪展，也都與「悟道」有關。在根本上，劍橋人相信人的真正成長必須來自自我的心靈的躍越。劍橋的教育，不像西洋油畫，畫得滿滿的；反倒像中國的文人畫：有有筆之筆，有無筆之筆。真正的趣致，還在那片空白。空白可以詠詩，可以飛墨，可以任想像馳遊，當然也可以是一片無意義的白。劍橋不把三年的課程填得滿滿的，一年三學期，每學期只有九個星期，它是要學生有足夠的時間去想，去涵泳，去自我尋覓。（改寫自金耀基《劍橋語絲》）

二、文章分析（佔 18 分）

閱讀框內文章之後，請分析：

(一)「漁人甚異之」的「異」和漁人發現桃花源有何關聯？

(二) 陶潛從哪些方面來描寫桃花源？

(三) 從中可看出陶潛嚮往什麼樣的理想世界？

答案必須標明（一）（二）（三）分列書寫。（一）、（二）、
（三）合計文長約250—300字（約11—14行）。

> 　　晉太元中，武陵人，捕魚為業。緣溪行，忘路之遠近。忽逢桃
> 花林，夾岸數百步，中無雜樹，芳草鮮美，落英繽紛。漁人甚異之。
> 復前行，欲窮其林。林盡水源，便得一山，山有小口，彷彿若有光。
> 便捨船，從口入。初極狹，才通人。復行數十步，豁然開朗。土地
> 平曠，屋舍儼然，有良田、美池、桑竹之屬，阡陌交通，雞犬相聞。
> 其中往來種作，男女衣著，悉如外人；黃髮垂髫，並怡然自樂。（陶
> 潛〈桃花源記〉）

三、引導寫作（佔 27 分）

　　老子說：「勝人者有力，自勝者強。」所謂「自勝者強」，
是指真正的強者，不在於贏過別人；而在於戰勝自己。現代社會
中，許多人喜歡跟別人競爭，卻不願好好面對自己，克服自己的
弱點。其實，只有改進自我，才能強化自我、成就自我。請根據
親身感受或所見所聞，以「**自勝者強**」為題，寫一篇文章。論說、
記敘、抒情皆可，文長不限。

101年度學科能力測驗國文科試題詳解

第壹部分：選擇題

一、單選題

1. **D**

   【解析】 (A) ㄧ、／ㄅㄧㄝˊ　　(B) ㄒㄧㄚ／ㄧㄚˋ
   　　　　 (C) ㄢ／ㄧㄢ　　　　(D) ㄓㄢ

2. **B**

   【解析】 (A) 以身作「責」→則　(B) 提綱「切」領→挈
   　　　　 (D) 因「漏」就簡→陋

3. **B**

   【解析】 (B) 切水果的刀

4. **D**

   【解析】 (A) 新鶯出谷：比喻人的歌聲，婉轉清脆，悅耳動聽，
   　　　　　　　如黃鶯在山谷間鳴叫般。
   　　　　 (B) 鬼斧神工：形容技藝精巧，非人力所能及。
   　　　　 (C) 郢書燕說：比喻穿鑿附會，扭曲原意。
   　　　　 (D) 郭公夏五：比喻缺漏的文字。

5. **A**

   【解析】 從「很像是球」選擇「浮滾」；再由「將要潰堤」判斷
   　　　　 出「洶湧」；至於「我獨自一人……四顧茫茫」當然只
   　　　　 有「蕭索」了

6. **C**

【解析】　關鍵字：甲、咬牙切齒、親密關係

　　　　　　乙、大小橫直數字、收拾生命

　　　　　　丙、肉身卸甲、膽固醇

7. **A**

【解析】　(A) 哂納：饋贈禮物時，請人接受的客氣話，亦作「笑納」。

　　　　　賜見：請見對方的客氣話。

　　　　　菲酌：粗劣的酒食，常用作謙詞。

8. **C**

【解析】　語譯：

　　　　　　《大學》這部書，是古代大學用來教人的方法。自從上天創生人類以來，則上天莫不賦予每個人仁、義、禮、智的本性。然而人的天資稟賦存在差別，於是人不都能知道並保有人的本性。如果有聰明智慧能保有人的本性，這樣的人出現，則上天必命他為人民的領導者，使他治理教化人民以回復善性。

9. **B**

【解析】　甲、東風暗換年華：初春

　　　　　乙、菡萏香銷翠葉殘，西風愁起：初秋

　　　　　丙、柳絲裊娜春無力：晚春

　　　　　丁、黃菊枝頭生曉寒：深秋

10. **C**

【解析】 英雄豪傑之胸懷，所以選先天下之憂而憂，後天下之
樂而樂；從討好、思念，所以選悠悠我心，豈無他人？
唯君之故，沉吟至今

11. **D**

【解析】 語譯：

四川境內有個姓杜的隱士，愛好書畫，所珍藏的
書畫有成百件，有戴嵩畫的牛一幅，他特別喜愛，用
錦囊玉軸裝盛起來，經常隨身攜帶，有一天曝曬書畫，
一個牧童看到這幅畫，拍手大笑說：「這畫的是角鬥的
牛呀，牛在角鬥時力量集中在角上，尾巴夾在兩條後
腿中間，但這幅畫卻畫成牛搖著尾巴鬥角，畫錯了
啊！」隱士笑了，認為牧童說得對。有句古話說：「耕
地應當去問奴僕，織布應當去問婢女。」這句話是不
可改變的。」

12-13為題組

12. **C**

13. **A**

14-15為題組

14. **B**

【解析】 (A) 助詞　　　(B) 指車　　　(C) 指寇兵

15. **A**

二、多選題

16. **DE**

【解析】 (A) 三天打魚，兩天曬網：比喻行事沒有恆心，時停時續，不能堅持。

(B) 一朝被蛇咬，十年怕草繩：比喻曾遭受挫折，後遇狀況就變得膽小如鼠。

(C) 千里送鵝毛，禮輕情意重：比喻禮物雖輕但情意深重。

17. **ABE**

【解析】 (C) 非日全蝕，乃日暮景象

(D) 非描寫白蛇，乃似白蛇的小溪

18. **BCDE**

【解析】 (A) 余光中

19. **CE**

【解析】 (A) 司馬遷主撰，為編年史之作

(B) 以項脊軒之變遷，來貫穿人事，以及自己當日讀書的興趣，家世興衰的感慨

(D) 儒林外史乃章回小說，非詳載科舉制度的史書

20. **AC**

【解析】 (A) 面對　　　　　　(B) 大概／危險、不安

(C) 借　　　　　　　　(D) 堅決／原本

(E) 愚笨、拙劣的／豈、何必

21. **AE**

【解析】 (B) (C) (D) 由近而遠

22. **CDE**

【解析】 (A) (B) 思鄉

23. **BCD**

【解析】 語譯：

我昔日少年讀書的時候，私自責怪顏回飲食粗劣的居住在簡陋的小巷裡，別人無法承受那一種憂苦，顏回卻不改變他的快樂。我私自以為雖然不願作官，但是去作抱關擊柝的工作，也可以養活自己，而且不會危害學習，為何如此困苦自己！後來到筠州，為了自己的生計辛苦勤勞，沒有一天不休息，雖然想拋棄凡塵俗事，解脫世間羈絆，寄託自己到道德的境地，但是俗事每每困苦自己而跳不出凡塵。然後才知道顏回所以甘心居於貧賤，不肯追求俸祿以供養自己的原因，是因為那會傷害學習的緣故。

第貳部分：非選擇題

一、文章解讀

劍橋的「心教」理念，就是讓學生擁有彈性的時間與空間，並建立一個充滿豐富意念景物的學習環境讓學生各自體悟提升。學生在「心教」的概念下，可以毫無束縛的按照自己心靈所向去學習，獲得真正的自我提升與成長，而使劍橋能培養出獨特想法、成為各個領域的箇中翹楚的學生；反觀台灣的教育體制，注重長時間的教學以灌輸大量的知識，使學生欠缺思辨能力，反而抹殺了許多有創意的英才，實應以心教理念作為借鏡。

二、文章分析

（一）因為驚於桃花源的景色，興起一探究竟的舉動，進而發現桃花源。

（二）由現實與心理兩層面描述：現實的農村環境簡樸、屋舍整齊、阡陌通暢、衣著樸素、成年男女工作勤實。心靈層面則呈現富足安定、老人小孩怡然自樂。

（三）從中可以看出陶淵明嚮往的仙境是心靈富足、勤樸寧靜的田園生活。小國寡民、男耕女織、老人與小孩可以自在快樂的遊玩。而由男女衣著，悉如外人，更可以呈現仙境中所追求的不在於物質享樂，而是心靈的安適滿足。

三、引導寫作

自勝者強

　　莎士比亞說：「你是獨一無二的，這是最大的讚美，還有誰能說得更有力？對自己都不信任，還會信什麼真理？」是的，唯有真誠面對自己，找出自己的弱點，進而相信自己一定辦得到而克服自己的缺點，戰勝自己的心魔，才能成就獨一無二的自我，到達成功的彼岸，而這也正是老子所謂「自勝者強」之真諦。

　　黑白混血、單親媽媽、隔代教養、勉強稱得上小康的家境，這些在一般人眼中極可能產生「問題兒童」的背景，卻造就了美國史上第一位非裔總統，歐巴馬。在青少年時期，歐巴馬曾用酒精和毒品麻醉自己，不願去思考「我是誰」的族群認同問題。但正如他的經典演講中所說，「假如我們等待某人或等待未來某刻再做，改變永遠不會到來。我們就是我們在等待的人。我們自己就是我們所追求的改變。」憑藉著這種從真實面對自我，從自我改變起的信念，在大學畢業後，他不在乎社會大眾的價值標準，放棄在紐約跨國公司的顧問機構擔任研究助理的難得職位與競爭機會，而到貧窮的黑人社區做組織工作，協助當地居民就業培訓、

改善環境等，切身的瞭解不同種族的痛苦，而這些草根經驗讓他更認清自己，克服自己的缺點，成爲他日後從政的重要養分，進而成爲美國史上第一位非裔總統。

我自己也深信「自勝者強」的道理。從小，我就對即席演說懷抱著異乎常人的狂熱與夢想，爲的不是戰勝別人，而是實現自我，告訴自己我能辦得到。想在三十分鐘的準備時限內，組織出一篇首尾完整，內容飽滿的文章，並字正腔圓的將它呈現得淋漓盡致並非易事。在國小時，我就曾因爲抽到不擅長的題目而敗北，但這反而更堅定我要面對自己的弱點，盡量準備過各種類型題目的決心。因此，我剪了一篇又一篇的報導，練習了一個又一個的題目，接受老師一次又一次的指導，除了專心在學業上，我必須比別人付出更多的時間與努力來追尋這樣的夢想。好幾個夜深人靜的晚上，我還在微弱的燈光下獨自搜索枯腸。

終於，在穩紮穩打的練習各種題目、提升演說技巧後，我不再害怕任何未知的題型，而且深切的體認到：我並非在與其他學校的對手競爭，而是在我自己能夠仰望的極限內期許自己做到最好！在戰勝自己的弱點後，我能輕易的在短時間內，上台侃侃而談，不僅在各大大小小的演說比賽中奪下了不少獎項，甚至拿下全國冠軍。這樣的信念，也讓我在往後碰到任何難關時皆無所畏懼，堅信著只要能夠努力精進自我，戰勝自己的弱點，所有的逆境就會迎刃而解，而能嘗到甜美的成功果實；而即便我們最後無法達到登峰造極的境界，亦可因爲戰勝自己而活得坦蕩快樂，問心無愧，而這正是人生強者的極致表現。

凱撒說：「你要出類拔萃，誰也抵擋不了你！」人生最大的敵人不是別人，而是自己。別人的失敗無法造就我們的成功，成日活在算計別人與競爭當中並無法得到真正的快樂與成長。在這個看似競爭的社會中，唯有正視自己的弱點，勇於面對並克服，才能真正提升自我，出類拔萃，造就無法抵擋的成功，爲自己的人生揮灑出彩色扉頁！（吳臻老師撰寫）

101年學測國文科非選擇題閱卷評分原則說明

閱卷召集人：蔡芳定（世新大學中文系教授）

本次參與閱卷的委員，均為各大學中文系、國文系、語文教育系或通識教育中心之教師，共計219人，分為16組，除正、副召集人統籌所有閱卷事宜外，每組均置一位協同主持人，負責該組閱卷工作，協同主持人均為各大學中文系、國文系之專任教授。

1月31日，由正、副召集人與八位協同主持人，抽取2000份答案卷，詳加評閱、分析、討論，草擬評分原則。每題選出「A」、「B」、「C」等第之標準卷各1份，及試閱卷各15份。2月1日，再由正、副召集人與15位協同主持人深入討論、評比所選出的標準卷及試閱卷，並審視、修訂所擬之評分原則，確定後，製作閱卷手冊，供2月2日正式閱卷前，各組協同主持人說明及全體閱卷委員參考之用，並作為評分時之參考。

本次國文科考試，非選擇題共三大題，占54分。第一大題為文章解讀，占9分；第二大題為文章分析，占18分；第三大題為引導寫作，占27分。

第一大題要求考生閱讀金耀基《劍橋語絲》中的一段文字後，解讀：為什麼作者認為「心教」才是劍橋教育真正的精華？並加以評論。評閱重點，在於檢視考生是否能解讀並評論作者的看法。凡能解讀並評論作者看法，內容充實，理路清晰，文字流暢者，得A等（7～9分）；大致能解讀並評論作者看法，內容平實，文字通順者，得B等（4～6分）；內容貧乏，評論失當，文字蕪雜者，得C等（1～3分）。其次，再視字數是否符合要求，錯別字是否過多，斟酌扣分。

　　第二大題要求考生閱讀陶潛〈桃花源記〉一段引文後，分析三個小題。評閱重點，在檢視考生，其一，是否針對「漁人甚異之」的「異」字加以發揮，並討論與發現桃花源的關係；其二，是否提及陶潛描寫桃花源的「自然景物」與「人們生活情狀」兩個面向；其三，是否針對陶潛嚮往的理想世界加以著墨。凡三小題皆分析正確深入，文字清暢，敘述清楚者，得 A 等（13~18 分）；三小題分析欠深入，文字大體平順，或三小題中二小題分析正確，文字敘述清楚者，得 B 等(7~12 分)；三小題中，其分析僅一題部分正確者，得 C 等(1~6 分)。另視是否分列小題作答，字數符合規定與否，及錯別字是否過多，斟酌扣分。

　　第三大題要求考生根據親身感受或所見所聞，以「自勝者強」為題，寫一篇文章，論說、記敘、抒情皆可，文長不限。評閱重點，從「題旨發揮」、「資料掌握」、「結構安排」、「字句運用」四項指標，加以評分。凡能掌握題幹要求，緊扣題旨發揮，論述周延，富有創意，能深刻回應引導內容，舉證詳實貼切，結構嚴謹，脈絡清楚，字句妥切，邏輯清晰，文筆流暢，修辭優美者，得 A 等(19~27 分)；尚能掌握題幹要求，依照題旨發揮，內容平實，思路尚稱清晰，且尚能回應引導內容，舉證平淡疏略，結構大致完整，脈絡大致清楚，用詞通順，造句平淡，文筆平順，修辭尚可者，得 B 等(10~18 分)；未能掌握題幹要求，題旨不明或偏離題旨，內容浮泛，思路不清，大部分抄襲引導內容，舉證鬆散模糊，結構鬆散，條理紛雜，字句欠當，邏輯不通，文筆蕪蔓，修辭粗俗者，得 C 等(1~9 分)。另視標點符號之使用與錯別字多寡，斟酌扣分。

【附錄一】

101 年度學科能力測驗
英文考科公佈答案

題號	答案	題號	答案	題號	答案
1	C	21	B	41	D
2	A	22	C	42	A
3	B	23	C	43	C
4	D	24	D	44	A
5	B	25	A	45	C
6	B	26	D	46	D
7	D	27	B	47	B
8	C	28	C	48	A
9	B	29	A	49	C
10	A	30	B	50	B
11	C	31	I	51	D
12	C	32	C	52	A
13	D	33	J	53	A
14	B	34	F	54	A
15	A	35	H	55	D
16	D	36	D	56	D
17	D	37	B		
18	A	38	E		
19	C	39	A		
20	B	40	G		

101年度學科能力測驗
國文、數學考科公佈答案

國　文		數　學			
題號	答案	題號	答案	題　號	答案
1	D	1	2	A	14	1
2	B	2	5		15	2
3	B	3	4		16	1
4	D	4	1	B	17	－
5	A	5	3		18	3
6	C	6	2	C	19	－
7	A	7	3		20	3
8	C	8	1,2,5		21	2
9	B	9	1,2		22	6
10	C	10	4,5	D	23	－
11	D	11	3,4		24	1
12	C	12	2,4		25	－
13	A	13	1,2,5		26	3
14	B			E	27	7
15	A			F	28	1
16	DE				29	2
17	ABE				30	1
18	BCDE				31	6
19	CE			G	32	3
20	AC				33	7
21	AE					
22	CDE					
23	BCD					

101年度學科能力測驗
社會考科公佈答案

題號	答案	題號	答案	題號	答案	題號	答案
1	C	21	D	41	D	61	B
2	C	22	B	42	A	62	A
3	D	23	C	43	C	63	B
4	B	24	A	44	B	64	C
5	B	25	B	45	C	65	C
6	A	26	A	46	C	66	C
7	D	27	B	47	A	67	A
8	B	28	D	48	D	68	D
9	A	29	C	49	B	69	D
10	A	30	C	50	A	70	C
11	C	31	A	51	A	71	C
12	B	32	B	52	B	72	A
13	C	33	C	53	D		
14	B	34	A	54	B		
15	D	35	D	55	C		
16	A	36	B	56	D		
17	C	37	A	57	C		
18	C	38	C	58	D		
19	D	39	D	59	C		
20	B	40	C	60	A		

101年度學科能力測驗
自然考科公佈答案

題號	答案	題號	答案	題號	答案	題號	答案
1	D	21	A	41	DE	61	B
2	C	22	E	42	BD	62	C
3	A	23	C	43	CE	63	C
4	E	24	B	44	E	64	B
5	A	25	B	45	D	65	B
6	C	26	D	46	E	66	A
7	D	27	B	47	C	67	BE
8	D	28	A	48	C	68	E
9	D	29	AE	49	AD		
10	D	30	DE	50	ABC		
11	D	31	ABD	51	C		
12	A	32	ACE	52	D		
13	E	33	CD	53	B		
14	D	34	CD	54	AD		
15	E	35	AD	55	B		
16	E	36	AC	56	AE		
17	D	37	AE	57	BC		
18	D	38	BD	58	E		
19	B	39	BD	59	D		
20	B	40	BE	60	E		

【附錄二】

101 年度學科能力測驗
總級分與各科成績標準一覽表

標準 項目	頂標	前標	均標	後標	底標
國　文	14	13	11	9	7
英　文	14	12	10	6	4
數　學	13	11	7	4	3
社　會	14	13	11	9	8
自　然	14	12	9	6	5
總級分	65	59	49	37	28

※五項標準之計算，均不含缺考生（總級分之計算不含五科都缺考的
　考生）之成績，計算方式如下：

　　　頂標：成績位於第 88 百分位數之考生級分。
　　　前標：成績位於第 75 百分位數之考生級分。
　　　均標：成績位於第 50 百分位數之考生級分。
　　　後標：成績位於第 25 百分位數之考生級分。
　　　底標：成績位於第 12 百分位數之考生級分。

【附錄三】

101 年度學科能力測驗
各科級分人數百分比累計表

	級分	人　數	百分比 (%)	累計人數	累計百分比 (%)
國	15	4,749	3.11	152,800	100.00
	14	13,749	9.00	148,051	96.89
	13	23,602	15.45	134,302	87.89
	12	27,332	17.89	110,700	72.45
	11	23,828	15.59	83,368	54.56
	10	17,822	11.66	59,540	38.97
	9	12,498	8.18	41,718	27.30
	8	9,145	5.98	29,220	19.12
	7	6,676	4.37	20,075	13.14
	6	5,199	3.40	13,399	8.77
文	5	3,572	2.34	8,200	5.37
	4	2,505	1.64	4,628	3.03
	3	1,466	0.96	2,123	1.39
	2	613	0.40	657	0.43
	1	37	0.02	44	0.03
	0	7	0.00	7	0.00
英	15	8,372	5.50	152,340	100.00
	14	14,193	9.32	143,968	94.50
	13	14,106	9.26	129,775	85.19
	12	15,187	9.97	115,669	75.93
	11	14,593	9.58	100,482	65.96
	10	13,795	9.06	85,889	56.38
	9	11,293	7.41	72,094	47.32
	8	10,740	7.05	60,801	39.91
	7	9,328	6.12	50,061	32.86
	6	8,421	5.53	40,733	26.74
文	5	7,980	5.24	32,312	21.21
	4	10,708	7.03	24,332	15.97
	3	11,303	7.42	13,624	8.94
	2	2,255	1.48	2,321	1.52
	1	62	0.04	66	0.04
	0	4	0.00	4	0.00

	級分	人　數	百分比 (%)	累計人數	累計百分比 (%)
數	15	5,867	3.84	152,640	100.00
	14	7,415	4.86	146,773	96.16
	13	9,499	6.22	139,358	91.30
	12	8,383	5.49	129,859	85.08
	11	10,884	7.13	121,476	79.58
	10	9,811	6.43	110,592	72.45
	9	11,446	7.50	100,781	66.03
	8	12,125	7.94	89,335	58.53
	7	10,729	7.03	77,210	50.58
學	6	13,512	8.85	66,481	43.55
	5	12,992	8.51	52,969	34.70
	4	16,120	10.56	39,977	26.19
	3	12,684	8.31	23,857	15.63
	2	9,188	6.02	11,173	7.32
	1	1,935	1.27	1,985	1.30
	0	50	0.03	50	0.03
社	15	5,902	3.87	152,600	100.00
	14	13,466	8.82	146,698	96.13
	13	22,574	14.79	133,232	87.31
	12	26,525	17.38	110,658	72.52
	11	29,112	19.08	84,133	55.13
	10	16,513	10.82	55,021	36.06
	9	12,255	8.03	38,508	25.23
	8	11,523	7.55	26,253	17.20
	7	6,982	4.58	14,730	9.65
	6	4,620	3.03	7,748	5.08
會	5	2,297	1.51	3,128	2.05
	4	773	0.51	831	0.54
	3	51	0.03	58	0.04
	2	3	0.00	7	0.00
	1	1	0.00	4	0.00
	0	3	0.00	3	0.00

	級分	人　數	百分比 (%)	累計人數	累計百分比 (%)
自	15	7,299	4.79	152,294	100.00
	14	11,973	7.86	144,995	95.21
	13	11,568	7.60	133,022	87.35
	12	12,316	8.09	121,454	79.75
	11	12,140	7.97	109,138	71.66
	10	13,605	8.93	96,998	63.69
	9	13,810	9.07	83,393	54.76
	8	14,786	9.71	69,583	45.69
	7	13,696	8.99	54,797	35.98
	6	14,230	9.34	41,101	26.99
然	5	13,494	8.86	26,871	17.64
	4	10,181	6.69	13,377	8.78
	3	2,922	1.92	3,196	2.10
	2	258	0.17	274	0.18
	1	11	0.01	16	0.01
	0	5	0.00	5	0.00

【劉毅老師的話】

　　我們出版歷屆的學測或指考試題詳解時，都會附上許多相關統計表格。不要小看這些表格，它們能讓你了解競爭者的實力，好勉勵自己要精益求精。

【附錄四】
101年度學科能力測驗
總級分人數百分比累計表

總級分	人數	百分比	累計人數	累計百分比
75	288	0.19	152,932	100.00
74	584	0.38	152,644	99.81
73	954	0.62	152,060	99.43
72	1,266	0.83	151,106	98.81
71	1,576	1.03	149,840	97.98
70	1,853	1.21	148,264	96.95
69	2,103	1.38	146,411	95.74
68	2,403	1.57	144,308	94.36
67	2,572	1.68	141,905	92.79
66	2,663	1.74	139,333	91.11
65	2,902	1.90	136,670	89.37
64	3,085	2.02	133,768	87.47
63	3,169	2.07	130,683	85.45
62	3,289	2.15	127,514	83.38
61	3,425	2.24	124,225	81.23
60	3,534	2.31	120,800	78.99
59	3,623	2.37	117,266	76.68
58	3,740	2.45	113,643	74.31
57	3,827	2.50	109,903	71.86
56	3,887	2.54	106,076	69.36
55	3,883	2.54	102,189	66.82
54	3,922	2.56	98,306	64.28
53	3,929	2.57	94,384	61.72
52	3,976	2.60	90,455	59.15
51	3,919	2.56	86,479	56.55
50	3,913	2.56	82,560	53.98
49	3,864	2.53	78,647	51.43
48	3,815	2.49	74,783	48.90
47	3,748	2.45	70,968	46.40
46	3,722	2.43	67,220	43.95
45	3,557	2.33	63,498	41.52
44	3,334	2.18	59,941	39.19
43	3,317	2.17	56,607	37.01
42	3,214	2.10	53,290	34.85
41	3,143	2.06	50,076	32.74
40	2,817	1.84	46,933	30.69

總級分	人數	百分比	累計人數	累計百分比
39	2,797	1.83	44,116	28.85
38	2,645	1.73	41,319	27.02
37	2,378	1.55	38,674	25.29
36	2,347	1.53	36,296	23.73
35	2,229	1.46	33,949	22.20
34	2,194	1.43	31,720	20.74
33	2,013	1.32	29,526	19.31
32	2,128	1.39	27,513	17.99
31	2,062	1.35	25,385	16.60
30	2,088	1.37	23,323	15.25
29	2,036	1.33	21,235	13.89
28	2,080	1.36	19,199	12.55
27	2,089	1.37	17,119	11.19
26	2,040	1.33	15,030	9.83
25	1,997	1.31	12,990	8.49
24	1,920	1.26	10,993	7.19
23	1,699	1.11	9,073	5.93
22	1,548	1.01	7,374	4.82
21	1,472	0.96	5,826	3.81
20	1,173	0.77	4,354	2.85
19	992	0.65	3,181	2.08
18	687	0.45	2,189	1.43
17	508	0.33	1,502	0.98
16	327	0.21	994	0.65
15	164	0.11	667	0.44
14	92	0.06	503	0.33
13	74	0.05	411	0.27
12	45	0.03	337	0.22
11	36	0.02	292	0.19
10	33	0.02	256	0.17
9	36	0.02	223	0.15
8	26	0.02	187	0.12
7	36	0.02	161	0.11
6	16	0.01	125	0.08
5	31	0.02	109	0.07
4	29	0.02	78	0.05
3	27	0.02	49	0.03
2	18	0.01	22	0.01
1	2	0.00	4	0.00
0	2	0.00	2	0.00

註：累計百分比＝從 0 到該級分的累計人數／（報名人數 - 五科均缺考人數）

【附錄五】

101 年度學科能力測驗
原始分數與級分對照表

科目	國 文	英 文	數 學	社 會	自 然
級距	6.15	6.38	6.57	8.55	8.21
級分	分　　數　　區　　間				
15	86.11 - 108.00	89.33 - 100.00	91.99 - 100.00	119.71 - 144.00	114.95 - 128.00
14	79.96 - 86.10	82.95 - 89.32	85.42 - 91.98	111.16 - 119.70	106.74 - 114.94
13	73.81 - 79.95	76.57 - 82.94	78.85 - 85.41	102.61 - 111.15	98.53 - 106.73
12	67.66 - 73.80	70.19 - 76.56	72.28 - 78.84	94.06 - 102.60	90.32 - 98.52
11	61.51 - 67.65	63.81 - 70.18	65.71 - 72.27	85.51 - 94.05	82.11 - 90.31
10	55.36 - 61.50	57.43 - 63.80	59.14 - 65.70	76.96 - 85.50	73.90 - 82.10
9	49.21 - 55.35	51.05 - 57.42	52.57 - 59.13	68.41 - 76.95	65.69 - 73.89
8	43.06 - 49.20	44.67 - 51.04	46.00 - 52.56	59.86 - 68.40	57.48 - 65.68
7	36.91 - 43.05	38.29 - 44.66	39.43 - 45.99	51.31 - 59.85	49.27 - 57.47
6	30.76 - 36.90	31.91 - 38.28	32.86 - 39.42	42.76 - 51.30	41.06 - 49.26
5	24.61 - 30.75	25.53 - 31.90	26.29 - 32.85	34.21 - 42.75	32.85 - 41.05
4	18.46 - 24.60	19.15 - 25.52	19.72 - 26.28	25.66 - 34.20	24.64 - 32.84
3	12.31 - 18.45	12.77 - 19.14	13.15 - 19.71	17.11 - 25.65	16.43 - 24.63
2	6.16 - 12.30	6.39 - 12.76	6.58 - 13.14	8.56 - 17.10	8.22 - 16.42
1	0.01 - 6.15	0.01 - 6.38	0.01 - 6.57	0.01 - 8.55	0.01 - 8.21
0	0.00 - 0.00	0.00 - 0.00	0.00 - 0.00	0.00 - 0.00	0.00 - 0.00

級分計算方式如下：

1. 級距：以各科到考考生，計算其原始得分前百分之一考生（取整數，小數無條件原始得分，再除以 15，並取至小數第二位，第三位四捨五入。

2. 本測驗之成績採級分制，原始得分 0 分為 0 級分，最高為 15 級分，缺考以 0 級分計。各級分與原始得分、級距之計算方式詳見簡章第 9〜10 頁。

101 年學科能力測驗各科試題詳解

主　　　編 / 劉　毅

發　行　所 / 學習出版有限公司
　　　　　　TEL (02) 2704-5525

郵 撥 帳 號 / 0512727-2 學習出版社帳戶

登　記　證 / 局版台業 2179 號

印　刷　所 / 文聯彩色印刷有限公司

台 北 門 市 / 台北市許昌街 10 號 2F　TEL (02) 2331-4060

台灣總經銷 / 紅螞蟻圖書有限公司　TEL (02) 2795-3656

美國總經銷 / Evergreen Book Store
　　　　　　TEL (818) 2813622

本公司網址　www.learnbook.com.tw

電 子 郵 件　learnbook@learnbook.com.tw

售價：新台幣二百二十元正

2012 年 4 月 1 日新修訂

ISBN 978-986-231-157-8